Extraordinary Jobs for

ADVENTURERS

Also in the Extraordinary Jobs series:

Extraordinary Jobs for

ADVENTURERS

ALECIA T. DEVANTIER & CAROL A. TURKINGTON

Ferguson
An imprint of Infobase Publishing

Ferguson
An imprint of Infobase Publishing
132 West 31st Street
New York NY 10001

Devantier, Alecia T.
  Extraordinary jobs for adventurers / by Alecia T. Devantier and Carol A. Turkington.
    p. cm.
  Includes bibliographical references and index.
  ISBN 0-8160-5852-0 (hc : alk. paper)
  1. Vocational guidance—United States. 2. Job descriptions. 3. Professions. I. Turkington, Carol.
II. Title.
  HF5382.5.U5D42 2006
  331.702'0973—dc22   2005019878

Ferguson books are available at special discounts when purchased in bulk quantities for businesses, associations, institutions, or sales promotions. Please call our Special Sales Department in New York at (212) 967-8800 or (800) 322-8755.

You can find Ferguson on the World Wide Web at http://www.fergpubco.com

Text design by Mary Susan Ryan-Flynn
Cover design by Salvatore Luongo

Printed in the United States of America

VB FOF 10 9 8 7 6 5 4 3 2 1

This book is printed on acid-free paper.

CONTENTS

ACKNOWLEDGMENTS

We would like to thank John Bales, Warren Clark, Scott Sleek, Barbara Turkington, Allen Miller, Elaine Bernarding, and Kathy Bennett of Cranmore Mountain Resort. We would also like to thank the staffs at Outward Bound, Vail Ski Resort, Cranmore Mountain Resort, Reading Municipal Airport, Pennsylvania Power and Light, and Rex Tomb and Neil Schiff at the Federal Bureau of Investigation.

ARE YOU CUT OUT FOR AN ADVENTUROUS CAREER?

Life is either a daring adventure, or nothing.

— Helen Keller

You drag yourself out of bed at 6 a.m., shower, grab a suit from your closet, and jump on the bus for the hour-long commute to your office, where you shuffle off to your cubicle and put in an eight-hour day.

What—that doesn't appeal to you?

If you can't stand the thought of sitting at a desk every day, gazing out your window at the world outside, watching it pass you by—then maybe you should consider an adventurous career.

Let's face it: Some folks just aren't cut out for the 9 to 5. But how do you know if you're more the bull-riding, smokejumping, fireworks-designing sort of person? Take some time to think about the kind of person you are and the sorts of experiences you dream of having.

First of all, ask yourself: *What am I passionate about?* Do you spend every waking moment thinking and dreaming about white-water rafting? Do you watch the wildfires out west on TV and yearn to be able to help? Do you fall so in love with an Outward Bound experience that you dream of someday teaching other students the same thing?

If you follow your heart, you're almost guaranteed to find a career you will love. In fact, almost every individual we interviewed for this book repeated the same litany—*I love my job. I love the independence.*

Sadly, adventurous jobs don't tend to pay very much—with a few exceptions. Yet while most adventure careers don't offer monetary rewards, to the folks who pursue those careers, it doesn't seem to matter. What those jobs do offer is something much harder to measure—and that's a job that lets your spirit soar and allows you to do what you love to do.

Of course, loving what you do is only part of having a successful adventure career. You've also got to be *good* at what you want to do. Most adventure jobs are so specialized that if you're going to go after one of them, you need to be really good at it. Whether you're thinking of becoming a bull rider or an adventure travel writer, you need to have the talent and the training to do that job better than most other people.

Next, how do you feel about risk? Adventure careers often entail quite a bit of risk. Many of these jobs could involve getting hurt. If you're logging, a tree could fall on you. Mountain guides can fall off mountains; ski patrollers can be buried by avalanches. Are you willing to face those risks?

Then there's the rest of the world. Chances are, if you're like most of us, you've inherited a bevy of *shoulds* about the kind of person you are. These *shoulds* inside your head can be a major stumbling block in finding and enjoying an adventurous career. Maybe other people won't be so happy with your career choice. You may hear complaints from your family and friends who just can't understand why you don't want a "regular job." If you confide your adventurous career dreams to some of these folks, they may try to discourage you. Can you handle their continuous skepticism, or downright disappointment? Other people often have their own *shoulds* for you too.

Or maybe you're having a hard time imagining a different path for yourself because of the obstacles you see. Maybe you're saying to yourself: "There's just no way I can follow my dream and make a living. I don't have the right education." "I don't have the right background." "I'm the wrong sex." or "I'm the wrong color." Patty Reilly, who you'll read about in this book, was one of the first women fishing guides back when she started out in the 1980s. Joan Feldman was the first cybersleuth when she started in the 1990s. Lots of men didn't want to be guided by Patty. Lots of men didn't want to refer cases to Joan. But both Patty and Joan refused to give up. Today they're both living their dreams—and they're both wildly successful at what they do. Patty built her own fishing guide business and travels all over the world, guiding men and women in fishing expeditions. Joan built her business on cybersleuthing and works on some of the biggest cases in the world.

Both are successful because they wouldn't accept someone else's assessment that they couldn't do what they loved to do because they were women.

Mike Moore had two strikes against him when he decided he wanted to ride bulls in a rodeo—he wasn't from the West, and he was black. He didn't listen to the naysayers who told him "black people can't be rodeo riders." He hung in there, and today he makes a successful living, doing what he wants to do—riding bulls.

If you get bogged down in the belief that you can't follow your dream because of what *is,* you take away your power to discover what *could be.* You lose the power to create a different future—an adventurous future.

Almost everyone we've talked to in this book has ended up with an adventurous job by a circuitous route. A few folks—like lobstermen, who tend to inherit their jobs—have always known exactly what they wanted to do, and did it. But for the rest of us, it can take years to work up the courage to actually do what we knew all along we would have loved to do. You'll find that living an adventurous life or having an adventurous career is usually built slowly out of a variety of different experiences.

You don't have to start big. You don't have to wake up one day and decide to climb Mount Everest. Start with the hill down your block or a small mountain in your state. Try unique educational experiences—take a climbing class. Try an internship or unconventional job, a summer job, travel, or volunteer.

Try not to think of learning and working as two totally separate things. When somebody hands you a diploma, you don't stop learning. School might be the best place to build up your fact-based knowledge; the rest of the things you do provide you with experience-based knowledge. You need both of those types of knowledge to forge an adventurous career. Remember that an adventurous career is an active experience: Take charge of your journey instead of relying on someone else's career path. Take advantage of the things you learn as you plan your next experience.

If you do decide to seek out an adventurous career, you'll almost certainly encounter setbacks. How do you handle adversity? How do you feel when you fail? If you've always wanted to be a race car driver, how are you going to feel if you can't seem to break into the business, or no one wants to sponsor you? If you can pick yourself up and keep going, you've probably got the temperament to survive the rocky road to an adventurer's career.

An adventurous career means growing through excitement and challenge. It's about learning to look at the world through curious eyes—to wonder what's on the other side of the mountain and actually go there to find out. By exploring your options for an adventurous career, you'll learn that work and play become the same thing. Push past your doubts and fears—and let your journey to adventure begin!

Carol A. Turkington
Alecia T. Devantier

HOW TO USE THIS BOOK

Students face lots of pressure to decide what they want to be when they grow up. For some students, the decision is easy, but for others, the choice isn't nearly so clear. If you're not interested in a traditional 9 to 5 job and you're an adventurous spirit looking for a unique way to make a living, where can you go to find out answers to questions you might have about these exciting, adventurous, nontraditional jobs?

Where can you go to find out how to become a Merchant Marine, traveling the high seas? What does it take to become a federal air marshal, helping to prevent terrorism? Where do you learn how to be a Secret Service agent? Is it really possible to make a living as a cybersleuth? Where would you go for training if you wanted to be a crime scene cleanup technician or a high-rise window washer? What's the job outlook for pyrotechnicians?

Look no further! This book will take you inside the world of a number of different highly adventurous jobs, answering questions you might have, letting you know what to expect if you pursue that career, introducing you to someone making a living that way, and providing resources if you want to do further research.

THE JOB PROFILES

All job profiles in this book have been broken down into the following fact-filled sections: At a Glance, Overview, and Interview. Each offers a distinct perspective on the job, and taken together give you a full view of the job in question.

At a Glance

Each entry starts out with an *At a Glance* box, offering a snapshot of important basic information to give you a quick glimpse of that particular job, including salary, education/experience, personal attributes, requirements, and outlook.

✓ *Salary range.* What can you expect to make? Salary ranges for the jobs in this book are as accurate as possible; many are based on data from the U.S. Bureau of Labor Statistics' *Occupational Outlook Handbook*. Information also comes from individuals, actual job ads, employers, and experts in the field. It's important to remember that salaries for any particular job vary greatly depending on experience, geographic location, and level of education. For example, smaller airports in towns and villages start their air traffic controllers at far lower salaries than they would make at much larger urban airports, which require a much higher degree of experience and skill.

✓ *Education/Experience.* What kind of education and experience does the job require? This section will give you some information about the types of education or experience requirements the job might have.

✓ *Personal attributes.* Do you have what it takes to do this job? How do you think of yourself? How would someone else describe you? This section will give you an idea of some of the personal characteristics and traits that might be useful in this career. These attributes were collected from articles written about the job, as well as recommendations from employers and people actually doing the jobs, working in the field.

✅ *Requirements.* Are you qualified? Some jobs, particularly those with the government, have strict age or education requirements. You might as well make sure you meet any health, medical, or screening requirements before going any further with your job pursuit.

✅ *Outlook.* What are your chances of finding a job? This section is based in part on the *Occupational Outlook Handbook*, as well as interviews with employers and experts doing the jobs. This information is typically a "best guess" based on the information that is available right now, including changes in the economy, situations in the country and around the world, job trends and retirement levels, as well as many other factors that can influence changes in the availability of jobs.

Overview

This section will give you an idea of what to expect from the job. For most of these jobs, there really is no such thing as an average day. Each new day, new job, or new assignment is a whole new adventure, bringing with it a unique set of challenges and rewards. This section provides a general overview of what a person holding this position might expect on a day-to-day basis.

The overview also gives more details about how to get into the profession. It takes a more detailed look at the required training or education, if needed, giving an in-depth look at what to expect during that training or educational period. If there are no training or education requirements for the job, this section will provide some suggestions for getting the experience you'll need to be successful.

No job is perfect, and there's no question about it: Adventurous jobs are dangerous. **Pitfalls** takes a look at some of the obvious and not-so-obvious pitfalls of the job. In many cases, the number of pitfalls far outweighs the number of perks. Don't let the pitfalls discourage you from pursuing the career; they are just things to be aware of while making your decision.

For many people, loving their job so much that they look forward to going to work every day is enough of a perk. **Perks** looks at some of the other perks of the job you may not have considered.

So what can you do *now* to start working toward the career of your dreams? **Get a Jump on the Job** will give you some ideas and suggestions for things that you can do now, even before graduating, to start preparing for this job. Opportunities include training programs, groups and organizations to join, as well as practical skills to learn.

Interview

In addition to taking a general look at the job, each entry features a discussion with someone who is lucky enough to do this job for a living. In addition to giving you an inside look at the job, the experts offer advice for people wanting to follow in their footsteps, pursuing a career in the same field.

APPENDIXES

Appendix A (Associations, Organizations, and Web Sites) lists places to look for additional information about each specific job, including professional associations, societies, unions, government organizations, Web sites, and periodicals. Associations and other groups are a great source of information, and there's an association for just about every job you can imagine. Many groups and associations have a student membership level, which you can join by paying a small fee. There are many advantages to joining an association, including the chance to make important contacts, receive helpful newsletters, and attend workshops or conferences. Some associations also offer scholarships that will make it easier to further your education. Other sources listed in this section include information about accredited training programs, forums, official government links, and more.

In **Appendix B** (**Online Career Resources**) we've gathered some of the best Web sites about unusual jobs in the adventurous area. Use these as a springboard to your own Internet research. All of this information was current when this book was written, but Web site addresses do change. If you can't find what you're looking for at a given address, do a simple Web search. The page may have been moved to a different location.

READ MORE ABOUT IT

In this back-of-the-book listing, we've gathered some helpful books that can give you more detailed information about each job we discuss in this book. Find these at the library or bookstore if you want to learn even more about adventurous jobs.

ADVENTURE TRAVEL GUIDE

OVERVIEW

Do you dream about spending your time spelunking in deep underground caves or dashing over hill and dale on horseback? Wonder how you can combine your love of adventure with a career? You might consider becoming an adventure travel guide.

These specialty travel tour guides organize and lead trips to exotic locations around the globe. Some do just the guiding part, while others guide and make all travel arrangements, including reserving lodging and dining, scheduling activities, and arranging for visas. Typically, guide positions go to the most experienced outdoorsmen and women. But being a guide isn't the only way to make a career out of a love of adventure: For nonguides, the adventure-travel industry offers a chance to work in an exciting environment with other adventure enthusiasts, with great perks and the satisfaction of being a part of their clients' unique, life-changing experiences.

As an adventure travel expert, you could work strictly in an office environment planning trip itineraries, making reservations for transportation, lodging, and activities, and selling the tours to travelers. If true action is more your style, you might be interested in being an outfitter or guide—working in the field, overseeing the travelers and guiding the tour activities. During the trip, you're responsible for educating the group on cultural customs, coaching individuals on

the basics of various adventurous activities, and overseeing the well-being and safety of all participants.

There are basically two types of adventure travel—*soft adventure* (for the more timid) and *hard adventure* (for the tough-minded adventurer). Soft adventure requires less physical ability and is usually suitable for families—trips including safaris, mountain biking, hiking, kayaking, skiing, horseback riding, diving, sailing, or cave exploration. Hard adventure requires a high degree of commitment from participants as well as advanced skills—such as mountain climbing, rock climbing, or white-water rafting.

Americans' interest in adventure travel hasn't yet hit its peak. This is creating a demand for people who can make the dreams of adventuresome travelers a reality. On the upside, because adventure travel is a fairly new phenomenon in the travel biz, there aren't yet a lot of requirements. However, while there is no specific certification required for adventure travel guides, some of the activities do require certification. For example, if you're going to be leading mountain trips, you may want to be certified in mountain guiding. Special training in emergency health care or first aid is always a plus. Universities and travel companies are just beginning to offer such programs.

If you're thinking of specializing in the business end of adventure travel, you should take business courses such as accounting, math, or computer science, as well as geography, history, and speech classes. A college degree in earth science, biology, history, or environmental affairs might give you an edge in those competitive hiring situations. If it's the action part of adventure travel you love, you should spend as much time as possible traveling and developing your physical fitness—not to mention developing special skills such as mountaineering, kayaking, or horseback riding.

Adventure travel guides need effective communication and people skills as they deal with a variety of people and situations. Contagious enthusiasm and experience in a range of adventurous disciplines will ensure a successful trip. It is crucial to be able to exercise good judgment under pressure and be resourceful when dealing with the emergency situations that are bound to arise. As a leader, you've got to be reliable and trustworthy to build your group's confidence so you can complete potentially dangerous activities.

In such a small profession, reputation is everything. Building and maintaining a good rapport with employers and coworkers is essential.

Pitfalls

There's no doubt about it—this job can be downright dangerous. It's also not the highest-paid career in the travel industry, and the paychecks can be sporadic. In fact, guiding represents a major responsibility, but that responsibility is not reflected in the wages. Pay depends on the length and difficulty of the trip, the guide's qualifications, and the company's budget. Guides also cite absence from family and friends as a pitfall of the job.

Perks

If you're interested in this job, it's because you love the outdoors, you love to travel, and you love people—all of which you'll have plenty of as an adventure travel guide. The job also affords a fair amount of freedom. How many people can say they get paid doing what they truly love to do? It can also be incredibly rewarding to help others attain life-changing personal goals they had thought were unattainable.

Get a Jump on the Job

If you think that someday you'd like to become an adventure travel guide, you can check out companies that hire people as apprentices, who, for minimal pay, help out on trips and thereby gain the

Mark Gunlogson, adventure travel guide

The lure of getting paid to do something he loved was the impetus that prompted Mark Gunlogson to begin his 15-year career as an adventure travel guide. Now vice president of Mountain Madness in Seattle, an adventure travel company specializing in mountain climbing, Gunlogson says that the appeal of adventure travel is definitely growing. Each year the company adds a few new programs and continues to hire more and more guides, he says. Although for the time being they focus on climbing and trekking trips, the company plans to expand into biking and kayaking as well.

"It's very rewarding to get people to the summit of a mountain," Gunlogson explains, "getting people doing something they had thought was outside the realm of possibility."

Gunlogson attributes much of the industry's recent jump in popularity to Jon Krakauer's book *Into Thin Air* (Villard Books, 1997), which details the tragic May 1996 Mt. Everest disaster that took the lives of eight climbers. The book generated quite a lot of publicity for adventure travel and has had a major impact in particular on the guiding group that led that expedition, Mountain Madness, Gunlogson says.

The industry is growing by leaps and bounds, in part because of strong interest from baby boomers, many of whom have always led very active lifestyles, and who are now empty nesters with disposable incomes—people interested in travel yet eager to avoid doing the same old boring thing on their two weeks of vacation. But because these travelers tend to be on tight schedules, they don't have the time or the inclination to plan their dream Peruvian fishing trip from scratch. And that's where an adventure travel guide comes in.

Of course, it's not all excitement and glamour. "This is a funny business," Gunlogson says. "There may be a lot of romance to it, but there isn't a lot of money. And it can be hard to get out of bed in the middle of the night to start a climb."

While there is enough work available to do adventure travel guiding year round, most experts suggest that this is an easy way to burn out. "Traveling all over the world is difficult, mentally and physically," Gunlogson says. "But you get to work with an interesting bunch of people who are free spirited and iconoclastic. It's unique and very rewarding."

expertise needed to become an assistant or head guide. Because many companies look for people with a Wilderness First Responder certificate, you might check into obtaining this training: It's a 72-hour course available around the country through Wilderness Medical Associates (http://www.wildmed.com) or through SOLO, an outdoor school (http://www.soloschools.com).

ADVENTURE TRAVEL WRITER

OVERVIEW

Picture this: One week you're floating down the Yangtze River. The next month, you're pony trekking across Exmoor in England. Two months later, you're huddling over a campfire on your way to Mt. Everest, or animal-watching in the Kalahari.

While most freelance writers produce articles from the comfort of their home offices, sitting around in their sweats drinking coffee and pecking away at their home computers, adventure travel writers carry their offices with them, ranging around the globe seeking new adventures to write about.

Most adventure travel writers started out as journalists for newspapers and magazines, eventually exchanging their corporate news desks and weekly paycheck for the much more independent, much less structured life—the uncharted waters of the self-employed. Yet while there is great personal freedom, there are still some basic requirements: Most travel adventure writers are tethered, however lightly, to a newspaper or magazine editor's approval and willingness to fund the trips.

Before a travel writer can fly off into the setting sun on another adventure, he or she must usually snag an assignment (or at least the whiff of an assignment) from a newspaper or magazine editor.

If you decide to become an adventure travel writer, before each trip you'll sit down and spend some time thinking about where you'd like to go next, or where your *readers* would like to read about next.

AT A GLANCE

Salary Range
$1,000 (newspapers) to $5,000 (magazines) per article.

Education/Experience
A four-year college degree (in any liberal arts major, English, or journalism) is helpful, along with experience writing for newspapers and magazines.

Personal Attributes
Curiosity, excellent communication skills, flexibility, attention to detail, independence, ability to meet deadlines, love of adventure travel.

Requirements
Writing talent and experience, ability to travel.

Outlook
Establishing a successful career in writing adventure articles for magazines and newspapers is a challenge. Only the most tenacious and talented writers will be able to make a good living by selling adventure articles for the limited printed resources that carry these articles.

Bird-watching in Patagonia? Float-fishing down the Snake River in Yellowstone National Park? Cattle-driving in Wyoming? After figuring out which editors might be interested, you'll send off a batch of query letters (or query e-mails) suggesting your idea. Halfway through this task, you might get a call from an editor responding to a pitch you sent out a few weeks ago. The editor didn't like your idea, but she likes your experience and your clips (samples of your articles). She has a different suggestion, and outlines to you the slant she wants the piece to have. If you both agree, she faxes you an assignment letter, and voila! Your next trip is set.

Typically, at least a quarter of your time will be spent in these sorts of home-office duties—paper pushing, record keeping, banking, tax filing, writing queries, and responding to editors. The other three-quarters of your time is spent in the glorious task of actually visiting far-flung adventure travel sites and then writing about your experiences.

To get there, though, you'll need to have gone to college and majored in some form of writing or communications. Hemingway might have been able to write articles about his international adventures without the benefit of a college education, but these days it helps to have a four-year degree related to writing, followed by some hard experience on a daily newspaper. A good liberal arts college can give you lots of general experience, and the newspaper will teach you how to write—and write well—on deadline. Once you've paid your dues, you can think about breaking in as a freelance adventure travel writer.

First, send a brief query about a place within the scope of the magazine's stated objective. If the editor calls to say she's interested, be sure you have two or three other ideas you can discuss casually. Show how you know the region.

Scale back your expectations. The world of travel writing is competitive, and it's unlikely that you'll break into the pages of the *Los Angeles Times* or *New York Times* on your first try. Instead, aim for medium-sized papers that use freelance material, or the smaller suburban papers near big-city markets. If you have a yen to write for the $2-a-word glossy travel and shelter magazine market, start small: Suggest an idea for the front-of-the-book sections made up of short clever items or product reviews. This type of story is really not much more than a fast-paced blurb, but the writer often gets a byline and a nice little check.

Magazine editors like to assign these midget pieces because there's little risk if you mess up—but if your work shines, she might be willing to consider giving you a longer assignment—and maybe even pay your expenses this time.

Next, you need to be sure to target your story to the right publication or market. Study where people in different groups like to go for their recreation—do families flock to dude ranches? Hip young singles hit the newest spiritual retreat? Seniors head out to California's wine country? What about the physically challenged, women-only, or high school teachers? Learn which audience the newspaper or magazine is writing for, and then construct a story idea and a focus that wows the travel editor and appeals to the publication's readership. If you're writing for *Modern Maturity* (the magazine for the American Association for Retired People), you don't want to suggest an article about cruising the Mediterranean with infants or how to keep your kids happy at Disney World.

Next, you need to have sharp eyes, an ear for accents, and a flair for characterization. Travel writing isn't just about buildings and landscapes, it's about people and places. Pay attention while you're researching the adventure so you can call up those sights, sounds, and smells for the reader.

Finally, never forget you're taking an adventure trip for your readers—not for yourself. Focus on what readers will want to do, so that they can do what you did when they trace the trip in your footsteps.

Pitfalls

Freelance writing can be lonely, enormously difficult to break into, and the pay

Bill Ecenbarger, adventure travel writer

A safari in Africa for the *Philadelphia Inquirer* started it all for Bill Ecenbarger, who'd been writing for the newspaper on a daily basis when he decided to leave to try the freelance life.

"The fact that I no longer had to show up for work every day gave me the flexibility to pursue travel writing," Ecenbarger explains. Soon he found himself looking for assignments that would get him to out-of-the-way places. "It was as much for the adventure of it as the money," he says. One trip led to another, and soon he had all the adventure he could handle.

Today, Ecenbarger's travel articles appear in a wide range of newspapers and magazines such as *Readers Digest* and *Islands*. His journalistic trips have taken him on a boat up the Yangtze River, on a 17-day freighter trip through the South Seas, and hiking the Milford Track in New Zealand, where he journeyed from a rainforest to a snow blizzard in six hours.

He loves adventure, but he still keeps his feet on the ground: He turned down the chance to bungee jump in New Zealand. "I look for adventure," he says, "not fright."

at first can be very low. Some people who are interested in travel find that endless voyages around the world eventually become lonely and stressful. As a self-employed writer, you have no benefits or paid sick leave. If you don't work, you don't eat.

Perks

A successful career as an adventure writer can take you to magical places all over the globe, where you'll meet fascinating people and have adventures. For very talented and prolific writers, the opportunity to earn a great salary while maintaining the freedom to travel and explore is an exciting combination.

Get a Jump on the Job

If you crave adventure and love to write, you can prepare early for this type of career. First, travel as much as your time and money (and family) will allow. At the same time, take as many writing courses as you can fit in, in both high school and college. If you have a school paper or literary magazine, get on the staff. Try submitting articles to teen magazines, and enter as many writing contests as you can. Choose a college with a strong writing program, and major in writing, English, journalism, or a strong liberal arts program. If you have an opportunity to study abroad in high school or college, grab it! In college, try to get as many writing internships as possible. If your college doesn't offer any, check around on your own at newspapers or magazines to see if they're hiring summer interns. On your own, write every day in a journal and practice your skills of observation.

AIR TRAFFIC CONTROLLER

OVERVIEW

If you've ever gazed out at the landing strips of a busy airport and wondered who's keeping all those planes straight, that would be the air traffic controller. Air traffic controllers are those folks up in the control tower who watch over all planes traveling through the airport's airspace. Their main responsibility is to organize the flow of aircraft in and out of the airport. Relying on radar and their own eyes as they peer through the tower windows, they closely monitor the airspace to make sure each plane keeps a safe distance away from each other, and guide pilots between the hangar or ramp and the end of the airport's airspace.

In addition, controllers warn pilots about changes in weather conditions, such as wind shear—a sudden dangerous shift in the velocity or direction of the wind that can cause a pilot to lose control of the aircraft.

As a plane approaches an airport, the pilot radios ahead to inform the terminal it's coming in. The controller in the radar room—just beneath the control tower—has a copy of the plane's flight plan and has already pinpointed the plane on radar. If the path is clear, the controller directs the pilot to a runway; if the airport is busy, the plane is fitted into a traffic pattern circling the airport, along with other aircraft waiting to land.

As the plane nears the runway, the pilot contacts the tower. There, another controller—who's also watching the plane

AT A GLANCE

Salary Range

Between $45,000 and $131,610, depending on responsibilities and complexity of the particular facility. Average annual salary, excluding overtime earnings, is about $95,700.

Education/Experience

A four-year college degree or three years of general work experience, military training in air traffic control, or a combination of both, followed by a combination of formal training at a Federal Aviation Administration (FAA)–approved education program and formal and on-the-job training.

Personal Attributes

The ability to concentrate is crucial because controllers must make swift decisions in the midst of noise and other distractions. Attention to detail, calmness, patience, and good communication skills are also important.

Requirements

Passage of the federal civil service exam, a written ability test, medical and drug screening, security clearance, and a week at the FAA Academy in Oklahoma City, which includes aptitude tests using computer simulators and physical and psychological examinations. For airport tower and enroute center positions, applicants must be less than 31 years old. Those 31 and over are eligible for positions at flight service stations.

Outlook

More positions will be available through 2010 as air traffic increases. Because of retirements, hundreds of job opportunities will be open each year for those graduating from FAA training programs. Competition to get into the FAA training programs will be keen, with many more applicants than there are openings.

on radar—monitors the aircraft for the last mile or so to the runway, delaying any departures that would interfere with the plane's landing. Once the plane has landed, a ground controller in the tower directs it along the taxiway to its assigned gate. The ground controller usually works entirely by sight, but may use radar if visibility is very poor.

The procedure is reversed for departures. The local controller informs the departing plane's pilot about conditions at the airport, such as weather, speed and direction of wind, and visibility. The local controller also issues runway clearance for the pilot to take off. Once in the air, the plane is guided out of the airport's airspace by the departure controller. After each plane departs, airport tower controllers notify enroute controllers who will next take charge, monitoring planes that are en route to their destinations.

There are 21 enroute air traffic control centers located around the country, each employing 300 to 700 enroute controllers, with more than 150 on duty during peak hours at the busier facilities. Airplanes usually fly along designated routes, and each center is assigned a certain airspace containing many different routes. Enroute controllers work in teams of up to three members, depending on how heavy traffic is; each team is responsible for a section of the center's airspace. A team, for example, might be responsible for all planes that are between 30 to 100 miles north of an airport and flying at an altitude between 6,000 and 18,000 feet.

To prepare for planes about to enter the team's airspace, the radar associate controller organizes flight plans coming off a printer. If two planes are scheduled to enter the team's airspace at nearly the same time, location, and altitude, this controller may arrange with the preceding control unit for one plane to change its flight path. The previous unit may have been another team at the same or an adjacent center, or a departure controller at a neighboring terminal. As a plane approaches a team's airspace, the radar controller accepts responsibility for the plane from the previous controlling unit. The controller also delegates responsibility for the plane to the next controlling unit when the plane leaves the team's airspace.

The radar controller, who is the senior team member, observes the planes in the team's airspace on radar and communicates with the pilots when necessary. Radar controllers warn pilots about nearby planes, bad weather conditions, and other potential hazards. Two planes on a collision course will be directed around each other. If a pilot wants to change altitude in search of better flying conditions, the controller will check to determine that no other planes will be along the proposed path. As the flight progresses, the team responsible for the aircraft notifies the next team in charge of the airspace ahead. Through team coordination, the plane arrives safely at its destination. Both airport tower and enroute controllers usually control several planes at a time; often, they have to make quick decisions about completely different activities. For example, a controller might direct a plane on its landing approach and at the same time provide pilots entering the airport's airspace with information about conditions at the airport. While instructing these pilots, the controller also would observe other planes in the vicinity, such as those in a holding pattern waiting for permission to land, to ensure that they remain well separated.

In addition to airport towers and enroute centers, air traffic controllers also work in flight service stations operated at more than 100 locations. These flight service specialists provide pilots with information on the station's particular area, including terrain, preflight and in-flight weather information, suggested routes, and other information important to the safety of a flight. Flight service station specialists help pilots in emergency situations and initiate and coordinate searches for missing or overdue aircraft. However, they are not involved in actively managing air traffic. Some air traffic controllers work at the Federal Aviation Administration (FAA) Air Traffic Control Systems Command Center in Herndon, Virginia, where they oversee the entire system. They look for situations that will create bottlenecks or other problems in the system, and then respond with a management plan for traffic into and out of the troubled sector. The objective is to keep traffic levels in the trouble spots manageable for the controllers working at enroute centers.

Currently, the FAA is implementing a new automated air traffic control system, called the National Airspace System (NAS) Architecture. The NAS Architecture is a long-term strategic plan that will allow controllers to deal more efficiently with the demands of increased air traffic.

There are additional jobs for air traffic controllers outside the towers and flight service stations, and in air route traffic control centers. Some professional controllers conduct research at the FAA's national experimental center near Atlantic City, New Jersey; others teach at the FAA Academy in Oklahoma City, Oklahoma.

Although most work for the FAA, a small number of civilian controllers work for the U.S. Department of Defense, while others work for private air traffic control companies providing service to non-FAA towers. Civilian air traffic control specialists work for the FAA in airports and control centers around the country.

Learning how to be an air traffic controller can be a daunting experience. It begins with seven months of intensive training at the FAA academy, learning the fundamentals of the airway system, regulations, controller equipment, aircraft performance characteristics, and lots of specialized tasks. To receive a job offer, you've got to successfully complete the training and pass a series of examinations, including a controller skills test that measures speed and accuracy in recognizing and correctly solving air traffic control problems. The test requires judgments on spatial relationships and requires application of the rules and procedures contained in the Air Traffic Control Handbook. The pre-employment test is currently offered only to students in the FAA Air Traffic Collegiate Training Initiative (AT-CTI) Program or the Minneapolis Community and Technical College Air Traffic Control Training Program.

In addition, you must either have been working full time for three years or completed four years of college. In combining education and experience, one year of undergraduate study (30 semester or 45 quarter hours) is equivalent to nine months of work experience.

Once you're selected, you're still not ready to go to work. Now you must spend 12 weeks at the FAA Academy in Oklahoma to learn the fundamentals of the airway system, FAA regulations, controller equipment, and aircraft performance characteristics, as well as more specialized tasks.

After graduation, you'll spend several years in progressively more responsible work experience, interspersed with considerable classroom instruction and independent study, to become a fully qualified controller.

Ted Johnson, air traffic controller

This job can be exciting at times," admits Ted Johnson, air traffic control manager at Reading Airport in Reading, Pennsylvania. "It's a good job, with steady work, although sometimes it can be boring."

At times, the responsibility of getting planes in safely can be quite stressful, he says. "But it's a lot less stressful since the installation of improved radar."

Johnson got his training in air traffic control in the military, along with about a quarter of the rest of the controllers in the country. Johnson—a controller for the past 29 years—chose to direct planes, not fly them, although about a third of controllers do have their pilot's license.

Controllers who fail to complete either the academy or the on-the-job portion of the training usually are dismissed.

Controllers must pass a physical examination each year and a job performance examination twice each year, and take continual drug-screening tests.

If you want to be a controller, you've got to be articulate, because you've got to give pilots directions quickly and clearly. Intelligence and a good memory are also important because controllers constantly receive information that they must immediately grasp, interpret, and remember. You've got to be decisive, because controllers often have to make quick decisions, and you've got to be able to concentrate in the midst of noise and other distractions.

When you first start, you begin by supplying pilots with basic flight data and airport information. If you can handle this, you advance to the position of ground controller, then local controller, departure controller—and finally, arrival controller. At an air route traffic control center, your first job would be to deliver printed flight plans to teams, gradually advancing to radar associate controller and then radar controller.

Controllers can transfer to jobs at different locations or advance to super-

visory positions, including management or staff jobs in air traffic control and top administrative jobs in the FAA. However, there are only limited opportunities for a controller to switch from a position in an enroute center to a tower.

Pitfalls

It's tough getting into the job, and once you get there the stress can be considerable. Because most control towers and centers operate 24 hours a day, seven days a week, controllers rotate night and weekend shifts. During busy times, you must work rapidly and efficiently. Total concentration is required to keep track of several planes at the same time and to make certain that all pilots receive correct instructions. The mental stress of being responsible for the safety of several aircraft and their passengers can be exhausting and incredibly stressful; the work environment can be very tense during busy periods.

Perks

Aircraft controllers earn relatively high pay and have good benefits, and they enjoy more job security than do most workers. The demand for air travel and the workloads of air traffic controllers decline during recessions, but controllers are seldom laid off.

Depending on length of service, air traffic controllers receive 13 to 26 days of paid vacation and 13 days of paid sick leave each year, life insurance, and health benefits. In addition, controllers can retire at an earlier age and with fewer years of service than other federal employees. Air traffic controllers are eligible to retire at age 50 with 20 years of service as an active air traffic controller or after 25 years of active service at any age. There is a mandatory retirement age of 56 for controllers who manage air traffic. However, federal law provides for exemptions to the mandatory age of 56, up to age 61, for controllers with exceptional skills and experience.

Get a Jump on the Job

If you are interested in airplanes and you think you'd like to work in the control tower of a big city airport someday, you can start down that road by getting your pilot's license. Air traffic controllers don't need to have a pilot's license, but it can help to be familiar with what it's like up in an airplane.

If you're interested in this career, many small municipal airports will arrange a tour of a control tower. This can help give you a sense of what the job is really like.

ARCHEOLOGIST

OVERVIEW

Have you ever wondered how the ancient Celts lived or what the Egyptians ate while they were building the pyramids? Digging up the answers to these questions is the job of archeologists, who study artifacts from past societies to try to discover and describe their cultures.

You can find archeologists in labs, classrooms, dig sites, or museums, working for colleges, the government, companies, and private clients. Archeologists who work in museums conduct research, prepare displays, and give public presentations. But the most common—and exciting—place to find an archeologist would be at an excavation site, whether it's in Israel, Mexico, China, or the eastern Mediterranean area, such as Rome or Crete.

Archeologists recover and examine historical artifacts such as ruins, tools, and pottery remaining from past human cultures, in order to determine the history, customs, and living habits of earlier civilizations. Research is a major activity, and various methods are used to assemble facts and construct theories.

Archeologists often work as an integral part of a research team. Most archeologists keep regular hours when not on a dig, usually working behind a desk. They read and write research articles or reports, either alone or in collaboration with other archeologists. Those employed by colleges and universities usually have flexible work schedules, often dividing their time among teaching, research, writing, consulting, or administrative responsibilities.

Many experience the pressures of writing and publishing, as well as those

AT A GLANCE

Salary Range
$31,200 to $38,990 to start.

Education/Experience
A Ph.D. or equivalent degree is a minimum requirement for most positions in colleges and universities, and is important for advancement to many top-level, nonacademic research and administrative posts. A master's degree allows you to teach in junior colleges and local educational societies. Knowledge of statistics, mathematics, geology, computers, and ancient and modern languages such as Latin and Greek is important.

Personal Attributes
Intellectual curiosity, love of history, creativity, objectivity, open-mindedness, excellent communication skills, ability to think logically, and systematic work habits. A strong desire to study ancient cultures and the flexibility to work in many different environments is important.

Requirements
A Ph.D. is required for most positions at the university level. A master's degree is required for junior colleges and local archeological educational jobs.

Outlook
Overall employment is expected to grow 9 to 17 percent through 2014, but archeologists face stiff competition for academic positions. Job opportunities vary depending on how much education and training you have. As construction projects increase, archeologists will be needed to perform preliminary excavations in order to preserve historical artifacts.

associated with deadlines and tight schedules. Travel may be necessary to collect information or attend meetings.

Other archeologists do fieldwork, living under rugged conditions and performing strenuous physical exercise. Archeologists on foreign assignment must adjust to unfamiliar cultures, climates, and languages.

It takes a lot of education to become an archeologist. Training in statistics and mathematics is essential for many archeologists, since mathematical and quantitative research methods are being used more and more in the field. The ability to use computers for research purposes is mandatory.

Some archeologists are interested in the study of ancient or classical civilizations, which require courses in art, architecture, and history. Others are interested in the study of historical periods, so you'd need to study history, material culture, and folklore. Some archeologists specialize in one area, state, or country; others specialize in one subject, such as cave drawings or burial sites, or one population, such as a specific Native American tribe.

Pitfalls

Competition for these jobs is tight, and many require travel and long periods of time in sometimes hostile environments. Excavating in all kinds of weather can be very hot or wet and uncomfortable. Salaries are rarely high for the amount of effort expended.

Perks

If you're interested in history or old civilizations, working out in the field to uncover long-abandoned artifacts can be tremendously exciting. There can be a certain amount of independence involved in working at a dig and an enormous amount of personal satisfaction in solving puzzles no one else has been able to piece together.

Get a Jump on the Job

To find out if archeology is the right career for you, it's a good idea to try to get some experience in the field. Many archeology students find that internships or field experience is helpful. Many local museums, historical societies, government agencies, and other organizations offer internships or volunteer research opportunities. A few archeological field schools instruct students on how to excavate historical sites.

Even teenage prospective archeologists can consider volunteering at a summer archeological field school to get an understanding of what goes on at an archeological dig. To find some opportunities:

- Check with your state archeological society—they may have an annual field school.
- Subscribe to the Passport In Time Traveler, a program in which volunteers work with archeologists in the National Forest Service on a variety of projects (Passport in Time Clearinghouse, P.O. Box 31315, Tucson, AZ 85751-1315; [520] 722-2716, [800] 281-9176; http://www.pastport intime.com).
- Check out the annual *Archaeological Fieldwork Opportunities Bulletin* (Kendall/Hunt Publishing Company, Order Department, 4050 Westmark Drive, Dubuque, IA 52002; [800] 228-0810; $11 plus $4 shipping and handling).

In addition, several organizations place volunteers and students into archeological field projects directed by professional archeologists. To check out these organizations, see Appendix A.

Mary Pirkl, archeologist

When I get a chance to learn a little bit more about a time and place, it's like being able to fit another piece into the puzzle," says Mary Pirkl, director of education at the Center for American Archeology at Kampsville, Indiana. For example, Pirkl explains that she once participated in an excavation on the Ohio River that uncovered a bottle once containing a Lydia Pinkham product. Pinkham had been an entrepreneur with a very successful "medical" business back east—yet this bottle had somehow found its way to Indiana. "After a little research, I learned that Lydia Pinkham's business had prospered, and her company sent products all over the United States, even back in the late 1800s," Pirkl explained, which revealed a great deal about the 19th century development of advertising, manufacturing, product distribution, and how people spent their money. "Learning about that bottle also taught me about people's ideas about medicine in the 1800s, and that's what it's all about for me," she explains.

The true excitement of archeology is being able to "watch" how people learn and change through time, Pirkl says, since the archeological record offers haunting glimpses into periods of time we will never truly understand because we simply weren't there. At the Center for American Archeology, Pirkl regularly teaches educational enrichment classes in local archeology and directs the summer field excavation program.

Pirkl, who holds a master's degree in anthropology, first became interested in a career in archeology as a child. "Throughout my life, I was interested in history, and reading. My parents got *National Geographic,* which fascinated me—learning how people lived their lives in other parts of the world. I simply loved learning and finding out who people are and what they do."

Although Pirkl assumed for a long time she'd become a professional archeologist who goes out in the field on digs, somewhere in her training she realized that what she really loved was educating the public about her field. Today, her job as director of the center means that "every day, my job is a little different, and the surprises in the field are always appealing." In addition, she loves working with a variety of people—everyone from first graders to senior citizens visit the center.

Although she enjoys being at an excavation site during nice weather, she notes that it can be hard work. While working in the lab can be tedious, working with the microscope can be fun. She particularly enjoys studying plant pollen back at the lab, which can reveal a great deal about the environment in which people were living. "Did you know that pollen from a pine tree looks like a set of Mickey Mouse ears?" she says.

Most of the excavations she's participated in have been located in Indiana, which has an extraordinarily rich history that began about 12,000 years ago. You may not find pyramids and golden statues in this state, but archeologists there have been able to piece together a lot of information about how ancient Indianans lived. Even something as simple as a fishhook found in an area where none existed before can reveal a lot about how ancient peoples lived.

She warns that you may not get rich in this field. "If you want to be driving a Porsche, you aren't going to get there as an archeologist," she laughs. Instead, archeology is a bit like the game of chess. "When you first start out, you have all these pieces of information, and each piece has its own special place, arrangement, and look. As the game progresses, you move these pieces around and examine them from many different angles—taking note of how they fit together as a group. By the end of the game, you've formed a strategy, looked at the information, and have made some decisions about what it all means. It's a terrific feeling when you've learned something that you didn't know before. For me, that's the best part of archeology."

BLIMP PILOT

OVERVIEW

Imagine getting a bird's-eye view of some of the country's biggest sporting events. That's what you'd have if you were piloting a blimp, which regularly fly over some of the most exciting national sporting events. Over the years, blimp crews have given TV audiences aerial views of the Super Bowl, World Series games, the Indianapolis 500, the Kentucky Derby, the America's Cup yacht races, Rose Bowl parades and games, and the 1996 Summer Olympics in Atlanta.

Several major corporations, including Fuji, MetLife, Pepsi Cola, and Monster .com, have commercial logo blimps that they use to advertise their products and services. But the granddaddy of them all is Goodyear. In 1925, Goodyear built its first helium-filled airship, the Pilgrim. Used for advertising, the Pilgrim visited rural areas all over the United States. During World War II, Goodyear blimps took to the skies to help in the war effort, escorting Navy convoys. From their position in the sky, blimp riders could watch the ocean's surface for rising submarines and then radio the subs' position. The big, slow airships were so effective that they worked with the U.S. Navy until 1962.

Since the Pilgrim, Goodyear has built more than 300 blimps—more than any other company in the world—and currently operates three blimps: the Spirit of Goodyear, based in Akron, Ohio; the Spirit of America, based in Carson, California; and the Stars and Stripes, based in Pompano Beach, Florida. Cruising at a

speed of 30 to 35 miles per hour at an altitude of 1,000 to 1,500 feet, the blimps travel more than 100,000 miles around the United States each year. When the blimps are flying long distances, crews try to cover 300 air miles a day, or about eight hours of flight time.

The pilot-in-charge (also called the chief pilot) has many duties other than

Dr. Jim Maloney, Goodyear blimp pilot

Like many little boys, Jim Maloney just wanted to follow in his father's footsteps. "My father flew for Goodyear before me," Maloney explains, and he always knew he wanted to pilot a Goodyear blimp. He even worked as a member of the blimp's ground crew when he was in high school.

"My dad always held the job [as a blimp pilot] in front of me like a carrot," he joked. Back then, the only requirement to become a blimp pilot was a high school diploma, but after high school, Maloney's dad told him Goodyear was hiring people with college credits. After his son earned a bachelor's degree, Maloney Sr. announced that people with graduate credits were applying for positions.

Figuring his dad couldn't tell him to get more education if he earned a doctorate degree, Maloney went on to earn a Ph.D. in electrical engineering—but with his degree in hand, now Maloney's father told him he was overqualified for the job!

Nevertheless, the younger Maloney persevered. He became a fixed-wing multi-engine heavier-than-air pilot, and finally, in 1983—more than 20 years after first joining the ground crew—Maloney got his Goodyear wings.

"I love meeting people and flying the blimp," he says. "I've been flying for over 20 years, and I still enjoy every flight." In his years piloting the Spirit of Goodyear, Maloney has covered numerous events, including Super Bowl games, World Series games, baseball playoffs, and Olympic contests. But of all the things he's done, it was an event at the Special Olympics in New Haven, Connecticut, that made the biggest impression. All of the participants in the stadium had disposable flash cameras, and as the stadium was darkened, everyone snapped a shot of the blimp at the same time.

Maloney suggests attending a college with an aviation-related program for blimp pilot hopefuls. You'll also need to earn a fixed-wing pilot's certificate with commercial instrument and multi-engine ratings. Next, apply, and keep applying. Most blimp pilots retire from Goodyear, and most openings are a result of retirements. Maloney anticipates one or two openings in the next five or six years.

"Continue your career while pursuing a job flying a blimp," he advises. "And continue working in aviation so that you'll be ready when there is an opening." Jobs in blimp flying can be tenuous. Jobs at Goodyear are tough to get, and pilots are required to pass a physical exam every six months to one year (depending on the position). If you can't pass the exam, you can't fly. For these reasons, a good fallback position is imperative. "Stay in school and get as much education as you can," Maloney advises, "so that you have something to fall back on."

simply flying the blimp. He or she is responsible for overseeing nearly every aspect of the airship—tracking crew and pilot work hours, monitoring maintenance, approving expenditures, and coordinating all trips. Before each flight, the chief pilot checks out the weather conditions before making the decision to fly.

Each blimp is accompanied by a ground crew of at least 15 people—riggers, engine mechanics, ground handlers, and electronics technicians, plus four pilots and a public relations manager. Each blimp also travels with several ground support vehicles, including a large bus, a tractor-trailer rig, and a passenger van. Since each blimp can only carry the pilot and five or six passengers, most of the crew travels on the ground. Crew members share the driving in addition to their other job responsibilities. They also take turns guarding the blimp, which is never left alone.

Because of the small number of blimps in the world, it's very difficult to become a blimp pilot. Goodyear trains all of its pilots, putting each new pilot through a six-month training period. During training you'll log more than 500 hours at the blimps controls before completing your check flight.

With your FAA lighter-than-air (LTA) pilot certification you'll not only be able to fly blimps, you'll also be a certified instructor. Eventually you'll help with the training of new pilots hired to work on your blimp.

Pitfalls

There are very few jobs for blimp pilots, but it's definitely worth all the work if you are one of the lucky few that gets a job. Blimps are on the road for six to eight months a year, which can be difficult if you have a family of your own. Even though Goodyear, for example, has flown for more than 50 years without any serious injuries, there's always that possibility.

Perks

Not only do you get a great view of some terrific sporting events, but you also get the chance to travel all around the country.

Get a Jump on the Job

Get your fixed-wing pilot's certificate with commercial instrument and multi-engine ratings, and consider working toward a college degree.

BOUNTY HUNTER

OVERVIEW

In the days of the Wild West, a bounty hunter was a gunslinger who earned big bucks riding the frontier ferreting out the bad guys for the reward on the "wanted" poster. Today's bounty hunter is called a fugitive recovery expert and works for professional fees, not bounties, which is why the term *bounty hunter* has fallen out of favor. But no matter what you call it, the fugitive recovery game is a shadowy, unregulated business devoted to finding and apprehending fugitives by whatever means it takes.

Here's how the system works: When a person is arrested and bail is set, the person can pay a fee to a bondsman, who posts his bail. The fee the person pays guarantees his promise that he'll appear for trial—but if he runs away instead, he forfeits the money he paid to the bondsman. When a fugitive skips bail, the bail bondsman hires a fugitive recovery expert to return a felon to the court, because the police don't have time to follow up on warrants. These experts typically receive a percentage of the bond as their fee.

So why don't bail bond agents go out and arrest their own felons who skip bail? They could, if they wanted to—but most don't want to. Almost 40 percent of bail bondsmen are women, many of whom don't want to be out there spending time arresting criminals. And the rest are just too busy to spend long hours of surveillance searching out crooks who skip.

AT A GLANCE

Salary Range

Successful bounty hunters can make more than $100,000 a year; part-timers can make $25,000 or more working some nights and weekends. Work is on contingency—if you can't find the fugitive, you don't get paid.

Education/Experience

Experience is the most popular way to learn, but there are a growing number of college certification programs and independent academies, including the National Institute of Bail Enforcement.

Personal Attributes

Street smarts, good people skills, patience, common sense, bravery, and intuition.

Requirements

Some states require a license; other states prohibit bail arrest (including Oregon, Kentucky, and Illinois). Florida recently passed a law in which it is a felony to say you are a bail enforcement agent/bounty hunter. Based on recent court decisions, the status of bounty hunters in Texas is still unclear.

Outlook

Competition is keen. Although there will always be warrants, criminals aren't always easy to find. Many bounty hunters hold other jobs to supplement their business. The most successful bounty hunters are national recovery agents, not limited to one city or county.

Under an 1872 Supreme Court decision, criminals surrender most of their civil rights when a bondsman bails them out of jail—in essence, the criminal becomes the bondsman's property. In most states, bail bondsmen and their fugitive recovery expert have broad powers that allow them to break into houses and drag their fugitive back to

John Smith*, fugitive recovery expert

Typical fugitive recovery experts spend more time researching on the phone and the Internet than they do busting down doors and slinging guns.

"I like to find people who don't want to be found," Smith says simply, explaining the allure of the job. Most of his time is spent tracking down small-time bail jumpers for a couple of hundred bucks each. On the job, Smith pays almost obsessive attention to detail. He doesn't carry a cell phone or pager for fear it might go off at critical time, affecting his concentration. On the job, he tries to blend in with the public, wearing jeans and a fleece pullover to hide his gun.

Most of the time, he just walks up to the front door and knocks—but sometimes he has to get a bit more creative. Once, Smith recalled, he tracked down the fugitive—but to actually arrest him, he bought a bunch of casino vouchers, hired a limousine, and told the fugitive he'd won a free casino trip. When the fugitive climbed eagerly into the limo, Smith and a partner jumped in the limo on either side and arrested him.

Although bounty hunters do carry guns and they're always ready to tackle their opponents, the professional bounty hunter prefers to be called a "fugitive recovery agent" and avoids gunplay and violence whenever possible. Most of the time, the fugitives come along willingly, Smith explains, which suits him just fine. "What really hurts [our image] is that we get these rogue fugitive recovery experts out there who go in and kick in doors." He's hoping that the government will step in and regulate his business to protect the professionals from rogue fugitive recovery experts.

* Not his real name.

court. Fugitive recovery experts spend most of their time tracking down small-time bail jumpers for a few hundred dollars apiece.

While they have considerable power to apprehend the baddies, that power is very narrow in scope: Professional fugitive recovery experts typically only apprehend a defendant who's skipped bail, which means they're only enforcing a bail contract on behalf of the bondsman. When a crook signs a bail bond contract, he basically waives his rights to the bonding agent—and if he doesn't appear in court, he's now fair game to a bail arrest throughout the United States.

Fugitive recovery experts often set elaborate traps to catch the convict off guard, using computers and phones to trace the felon. If you're a fugitive recovery expert on a felon's trail, often you'll only need to walk up the front drive and knock on his door. You can break in if you know beyond a reasonable doubt that it's where the crook lives—but you can't go into somebody else's house on a fishing expedition, hoping to find the crook playing poker with his buddies. Although they are allowed to use *any means necessary* to capture a criminal, fugitive recovery experts only use violence as a last resort, in self-defense. When you're doing your job, you can't expect the police to help you. Many officers will do a "keep the peace" call, to stand by in the cruiser for effect. But many departments advise their officers against taking part in what is, in fact, a private arrest.

Once you've arrested the fugitive, you're done. You can't arrest anybody else—until a bonding agent hires you for another case.

However, bounty hunting is more than getting clients, finding their felons, turning them in and collecting your fee—even though it will often seem that simple. You've got to be good at *skip tracing* (locating a fugitive) and apprehending him safely, but you'll also need other skills in surveillance, negotiating, interviewing, and detecting. Knowing the law is also important. Experts—especially those who cross state borders—need to know if it's a felony to have pepper gas, if it's legal to own handcuffs—and what to do if a small child appears as you're handcuffing his father, the only guardian at the scene.

You're also running your own business, so you've also got to be good at marketing and advertising your services, networking, and research. Because safety is a priority, bondsmen try to hire fugitive recovery experts with a long history of safety and results.

Pitfalls

Apprehending fugitives can be dangerous. No amount of training or help can guarantee your safety while taking a defendant into custody, even for the most minor criminal offense.

Perks

The money can be excellent and the personal freedom and challenge appeals to some.

Get a Jump on the Job

As you might imagine, there really aren't any courses on the subject, and you can't major in "bounty hunter" in college. However, you can take college courses in criminal justice, along with a variety of other classes to give you a broad background.

BULL RIDER

OVERVIEW

One… two… three… four… five… six… seven… *eight seconds!* That's a full *day* on the job for a bull rider. But for the rider strapped to a 2,000-pound bull, it might seem more like an eternity. For the fans in the stands, it's those eight seconds of heart-pounding excitement that make bull riding one of rodeo's most popular events.

The object of bull riding is simple: You've got to stay on board for eight seconds. A flat braided rope is wrapped around the bull's chest; one end of the rope is threaded through a loop on the other end of the rope, and pulled tight. Riders hold onto the rope, wrapping it around their hand or weaving it through their fingers. With a nod of the head signaling that the rider is ready, the chute opens and the bull rockets out of the gate.

That's when the clock starts. The bull rider must hold on with only one hand for eight seconds while the bull bucks, jumps, spins, or kicks, trying to get the rider off his back. If the rider's free hand touches himself or the bull, the rider is disqualified.

To protect themselves, all bull riders wear several pieces of protective clothing. Most important is a glove on their riding hand (the hand holding the rope), which helps prevent rope burn and makes it easier for the rider to hang onto the rope. A protective vest (made from the same material as bulletproof vests) protects the rider's upper body from the bull's hooves and horns. Riders also wear spurred boots, chaps, and a cowboy hat. Some riders wear a helmet and/or a face mask.

Even with the precautions that riders take, injuries happen. It's not *if* a bull rider will be injured, it's *when*—and how badly. The most frequent injury is a concussion, but shoulder injuries are also very common. At some point during a career, almost every rider will suffer from some type of groin injury.

Before climbing onto a one-ton bull and competing against some of the best riders in the country, you'll want to get some training. Some riders start out participating in small, local competitions,

Mike Moore, bull rider

My family never said `you can't do this, it's not possible,' " says bull rider Mike Moore, who isn't your typical bull rider. "My grandfather lived in the country and had some horses, and I always wanted to be a cowboy." But unlike many rodeo competitors who start riding when they were very young, Moore, who grew up 45 miles south of Chicago, didn't start riding bulls until the summer he turned 17. Even though everyone except his family told him that a black guy from Illinois couldn't be a cowboy, Moore knew that was what he wanted to do.

Luckily for him, not only did his family believe in him, but the dean of students at his junior high school was a stock contractor—someone who owns and leases animals to the rodeo. "I pestered him as much as I could, just to be around him," Moore said.

That determination paid off. The summer Moore turned 15, he was hired on to work on the stock contractor's rodeo crew setting up for rodeo events and taking care of the livestock. The next summer he started riding broncos and was hooked. It wasn't until the following summer Moore climbed onto a bull for the first time. "I'd never experienced anything like it," he said. He described the whole experience as "a rush."

After high school, Moore earned an associate's degree in animal science and a bachelor's degree in elementary education at a college in Wyoming. Today, Moore rides bulls for a living back home in Illinois, where he can be close to his family. In addition to the great people on the rodeo circuit, Moore enjoys being his own boss. "I can set up my own schedule and do what rodeos I want to do."

"Going to a good, quality school is very important. Learn how to do it right, from someone who knows… And when you're done [training], leave with a positive attitude and go at it wholeheartedly. Be prepared to be hurt, because no matter how good a rider you are, eventually it will happen."

learning from more experienced riders. Others attend a bull-riding school. Depending on the school, students might have the opportunity to learn from a former champion bull rider. Many riders learn through a combination of bull-riding school and competitions.

Top riders encourage people just starting out to get the best training that they can. This can spell the difference between a champion rider and someone who's just a competitor, but good training also teaches riders how to do things safely and correctly, which can mean the difference between life and death.

When your riding days are over, you might choose to stay active in bull riding by becoming a judge or an announcer or by opening a bull-riding school of your own. Some veterans become stock contractors—those who own bulls and rent them for bull-riding events.

Pitfalls

One of the biggest pitfalls in bull riding is the injuries, which can be so bad that they can end your career, or maybe even your life. Until you start winning a lot of competitions, it might be difficult to support yourself with only your rodeo prizes.

Perks

You'll have the opportunity to travel regionally to different rodeos and bull-riding events, or even compete throughout the United States, participating in one of the most popular spectator sports in the country.

Get a Jump on the Job

Look for programs, schools, and other opportunities where you can learn the basics of bull riding. There are several organizations for bull riders under 18. Contact the American Junior Rodeo Association (http://www.ajra.org), the National High School Rodeo Association (http://www.nhsra.org), or the National Little Britches Rodeo Association (http://www.nlbra.com). In addition to giving aspiring bull riders valuable experience, these organizations offer young riders the chance to win cash prizes and scholarships.

CHIMNEY SWEEP

OVERVIEW

Chimney sweeps don't always wear a top hat, tie, and tails to clean chimneys nowadays—but they do earn a pretty good living making sure chimneys are safe and clean. Gone are the days of shimmying through tight spaces and climbing into smoky, dark chimneys carrying a long-handled brush. Today's chimney sweep (they prefer *chimney professional* or *chimney technician*) is a certified safety professional who installs, cleans, and maintains heating systems and their chimneys, evaluates performance, prescribes changes to improve performance, and educates the consumer about chimney safety.

In particular, wood-burning heating systems require careful monitoring and skillful operation because burning fuels causes a buildup of highly combustible creosote, which can cause a chimney fire. The National Fire Protection Association (NFPA) recommends all chimneys and vents be inspected annually and cleaned if needed, because each year, there are about 23,600 residential fires related to chimneys. Another 5,500 fires each year are attributed to chimneys and chimney connectors serving heating systems burning liquid and other fuels.

The basic job of a chimney sweep is to clean chimneys—removing highly combustible creosote produced by burning wood and wood products. They also get rid of bird and animal nests, leaves, and other debris that can block emissions

from a home heating appliance. Sweeps also act as on-the-job fire prevention specialists, constantly on the lookout for unsafe conditions that can cause home fires or threaten residents with dangerous or unhealthy indoor air quality.

Chimney inspections often reveal hidden problems with a chimney structure that could be potentially hazardous. Mechanical sweeping of chimneys not only removes layers of creosote from the chimney surface, it removes the resulting loose soot and creosote from the chimney, fireplace, or wood stove.

But chimney sweeps don't concentrate just on fireplaces. When gas and oil burn in vented heating systems, dangerous

Mike Polyak, chimney sweep

Mike Polyak has been a Reading, Pennsylvania, sweep for the past 30 years, founding Polyak Services in 1973. Armed with a strong masonry background in chimney and fireplace building and repair, brick and block work, and brick and stone pointing, Polyak realized that he needed to specialize in some aspect of home construction that wasn't so competitive. With a yen to build a business, Polyak recognized that *cleaning* chimneys—not just building them—could make for a pretty good business.

"I realized that you'd always need someone to clean and service chimneys," he says, "and being able to repair or build chimneys would only expand the business."

Polyak began professionally inspecting, cleaning, and relining fireplaces and chimneys in 1978. In 1990, he expanded into the air duct cleaning market, and in 2003 introduced a professional residential and commercial dryer vent cleaning service.

One of the hardest parts of the job, Polyak says, is keeping a steady flow of work. Business tends to get incredibly busy in the fall, as homeowners realize they need to have their chimneys cleaned in time for the first cold days of winter. "That's the high pressure time," Polyak says, "and you get a lot of calls from people who waited to the last minute to get their chimneys cleaned." But in early spring, work slows down again.

Although keeping a chimney clean and in good repair is a vital safety issue, no one is required to have a chimney inspected—unlike in Europe, where chimney sweeping is regulated by the state, and homeowners must have their local sweep attend to their chimney each year.

Certified by the Chimney Safety Institute of America, Polyak is also a member of the National Chimney Sweep Guild and the Pennsylvania Guild of Chimney Sweeps. Having these designations promotes professionalism, Polyak says. "It's what separates us from the fly-by-nighters who service chimneys with tools from the back of a station wagon."

Despite the hectic seasonal nature of the work and the serious liability issues and responsibilities he carries for his clients, Polyak truly loves his job. "It's actually very satisfying to help people have a properly functioning chimney or fireplace," he explains. "It's very rewarding knowing that you're helping to keep families safe."

fumes (including carbon monoxide) are released into a chimney through a connector pipe. Chimneys funnel these fumes out of the living area and create the flow of air that provides the proper air and fuel mixture for efficient operation of a heater.

The best sweeps earn certification from the Chimney Safety Institute of America by passing a 100-question exam with a score of 80 or higher, based on standard chimney service practices and applicable fire safety codes. Certification is valid for three years from the exam date. Most people can't pass the test without studying the reference manual *Successful Chimney Sweeping* and the 2003 version of NFPA 211.

While sweeping today's chimneys and caring for heating systems can be a fairly complicated job, the chimney service trade is not yet regulated, nor are chimney sweeps licensed in most states. Just about anybody can open a chimney service business with a small amount of cash, which means that almost anyone—

without education, training, experience, or even a working knowledge of tools or equipment—can become a chimney sweep. For this reason, a number of states are currently considering licensing chimney sweeps. Today, some towns license chimney sweeps, requiring that sweeps have the CSIA certification. Sweeps must also understand the most recent NFPA standards as well as the specifics of state and local codes covering their geographic area.

While many sweeps first learn the job as an apprentice, you can get a head start by attending the CSIA National Chimney Sweep Training School—an in-depth, six-day course that teaches the basic skills chimney professionals use every day. (For contact information, see Appendix A.) The course helps students learn the most up-to-date tools, technologies, and standards, combining classroom training with hands-on experience at the CSIA Technology Center and in actual customers' homes. After completing the program, students will have the knowledge and skills to handle the basic work of a chimney service professional.

Pitfalls

Although modern equipment has improved working conditions, this can still be a dusty, dirty job. Chimney sweeps must wear protective clothing including overalls and face masks. The work involves much standing, kneeling, and bending, and some lifting.

The responsibility and liability also can be burdensome; an imperfectly cleaned or repaired chimney or vent could prove dangerous or fatal to a homeowner.

Perks

Chimney sweeps can earn very good salaries and the work generally suits those who are independent and self-motivated.

Get a Jump on the Job

The best way to learn this trade is to get out there and get some on-the-job experience. Contact a local certified sweep and offer to work during the busy season (autumn) in any position. Most business owners say they like to hire people without lots of experience so they can train them properly, right from the beginning.

COAST GUARD OFFICER

OVERVIEW

As a member of the U.S. Coast Guard, you'll join 38,000 active-duty men and women and 8,000 reservists who live and work by the motto *Semper Paratus*: Always Ready. And ready they are—ready to rescue people in distress, clear waterways, protect natural resources, keep America's shores and waterways safe, and help keep drugs from crossing our borders.

During an average day, Coast Guard personnel will conduct 109 search and rescue missions, save 10 lives, help 192 people in distress, seize 169 pounds of marijuana and 306 pounds of cocaine, intercept 14 illegal immigrants, and board 144 vessels.

If all of that stuff sounds like fun to you, a Coast Guard career might be for you. Depending on your interests and ability, you might choose to focus on safety and law enforcement, enforcing laws and rescuing people in trouble on waterways. You might decide to work in maritime patrols, helping sailors navigate waterways or inspecting ships to make sure they're seaworthy. Perhaps you'd like to serve on an environmental response team. If you're a techno wizard, you might become a technician, operating advanced electronics, telecommunications, and computer systems. If paper is more your thing, you can work in accounting or office management.

All positions in the Coast Guard—including combat roles—are open to women.

There are two ways to get into the Coast Guard: as an enlistee or as an officer. If you choose the enlistee route, you'll spend eight weeks in and out of the classroom at boot camp at the U.S. Coast Guard Training Center in Cape May, New Jersey. There

Seaman Scott Wakefield, U.S. Coast Guard

The opportunities are fantastic," says Seaman Scott Wakefield. "Boot camp is the worst part, but once you get through it, you have a lot of possibilities." With all the different opportunities available, Wakefield says, "there really is something for everyone, especially if you like the water." Nine months after graduating from basic training, Wakefield is now stationed aboard the Coast Guard cutter *Acacia*.

"I went to college for a while, but really dragged my feet about what to do," Wakefield explains. Now studying marine science technology, he'll be able to earn his degree through correspondence and online classes while he's serving on board the *Acacia*. In addition to the training he receives in the Coast Guard, Wakefield will have earned $34,000 he can use to pursue other educational opportunities when his duty to the Coast Guard is complete.

"[Working on] the *Acacia* is exciting; it's always something new," Wakefield says. On a typical day, his main job is to service buoys around the Great Lakes.

"Understand that you'll start at the bottom," he cautions. "You'll do monotonous jobs and tiresome work [like painting, cleaning, and even mowing lawns when you're in port]. But keep in mind the possibilities that you'll have. You can advance fairly quickly. If you're ambitious, you'll go far."

you'll learn first aid, fire fighting, seamanship, and how to operate an M-1 carbine rifle. You'll have physical fitness classes every day, in addition to pool time, where you'll learn water survival skills. Military drill is an important part of the training too.

If you want to be an officer in the Coast Guard, you can attend the Coast Guard Academy in New London, Connecticut, after high school. About 300 freshmen start at the academy each fall, majoring in engineering, naval architecture, computer analysis, or marine environmental science. Tuition at the academy is free, and you'll even earn a modest paycheck while you're in school. When you graduate, you'll receive a commission as an ensign, and you'll be required to serve in the Coast Guard for five years. The application deadline for the academy is January 31 each year, and congressional nominations are not required.

If you're already a college graduate, you can instead attend 17 weeks of Officer Candidate School (OCS) in New London. After you finish OCS, you'll be commissioned as an ensign in the Coast Guard Reserve, where you'll need to complete three years of active duty.

On the other hand, if you decide a full-time career in the Coast Guard isn't quite right for you, there's always the Coast Guard Reserves or the Coast Guard Auxiliary. Reservists serve one weekend a month, and two weeks every year, and work with active duty personnel, performing the same jobs. The Coast Guard Auxiliary includes more than 35,000 men and women volunteers who help the Coast Guard with public education, safety patrols, vessel safety checks, environmental protection, youth programs, and search and rescue.

Pitfalls

Depending on your specialty or your assignment, you might need to relocate, away from family and friends. While the chance that you could be sent to another country is slim, Coast Guard personnel can be deployed to a war zone if needed—which means risk of being injured or killed in the line of duty. Throughout history, combat-related deaths for Coast Guard personnel have been low, but it does happen.

Perks

Coast Guard personnel enjoy lots of benefits, including steady income, health and dental insurance, two-and-a-half days of paid vacation a month (30 days a year), and a monthly allowance for uniforms, food, and housing. The government will also help pay for additional college or vocational technical training.

Get a Jump on the Job

Check your local library or bookstore for books to help your prepare for the entrance exam (ASVAB). Prepare for the physical requirements of Coast Guard training. Men need to do 29 push-ups and 38 sit-ups in one minute; run a mile and a half in 12:51; and get a "sit and reach" score of at least 16.50. Women need to do 23 push-ups and 32 sit-ups in one minute; run a mile and a half in 15:26; and get a "sit and reach" score of at least 19.25. All candidates are required to jump off a five-foot platform into the pool, swim 100 meters, and tread water for five minutes.

COMMERCIAL DIVER

OVERVIEW

When you work as a commercial diver, you'll get up in the morning and put on a suit and head off to the office, just like millions of other men and women in all walks of life—with two exceptions. First, the suit you'll be slipping into is a wet suit, and second, your office will be located somewhere underwater.

Commercial divers are underwater construction workers. They do many of the same jobs as traditional construction workers—they just do them underwater. In many ways, a commercial diver needs to be a jack-of-all-trades. They construct, maintain, and repair barges, dams, bridges, piers, sewage pipes, and pipelines. They install and repair intake valves and other underwater parts at water plants, paper mills, nuclear power plants, and sewage treatment plants. They repair ships while they're still in the water, or work on search and recovery of sunken vessels.

Depending on their training, skills, and interests, commercial divers can work either inland or offshore. Offshore divers work in a gulf or the open ocean, concentrating on building, maintaining, and repairing oil rigs, wells, and pipelines. About 60 percent of U.S. commercial divers work in the Gulf of Mexico. Inland commercial divers could be hired to work on any underwater structure in a lake, river, or other inland waterway.

Because their job site is so far under water, these divers need to be resourceful and think quickly, always ready to handle

AT A GLANCE

Salary Range

Beginning divers start at $8 to $9 an hour. Salaries increase with experience and time on the job. Inland divers generally earn more than offshore divers. Experienced divers with trade skills can earn $35,000 to $70,000 a year.

Education/Experience

Many employers look for divers with a certificate from a school accredited by the Association of Commercial Diver Educators (ACDE). Most dive schools require a high school diploma or GED. Some schools may require SCUBA certification.

Personal Attributes

Must like the water, and be dependable, resourceful, quick-thinking, able to work as a part of a team, and trust coworkers.

Requirements

You must pass a thorough medical exam before beginning dive school. Employers may also require annual checkups. Some jobs may require union membership.

Outlook

The outlook for entry-level offshore diving jobs is good. The need for inland divers should increase as existing bridges, water treatment plants, dams, and other underwater structures age and need repair. Inland divers will also be needed for the construction of new structures.

unexpected problems using the tools and supplies they have on hand. And keep in mind, all this must be done underwater, in cold temperatures, with low visibility.

For commercial divers, the workday is as varied as the jobs they perform, especially for inland divers. To take advantage of good diving weather or simply because a job needs to be completed, they may work

Gary Mason, inland commercial diver

Every day is different for commercial divers," says inland commercial diver Gary Mason. "Each job brings new challenges and requires different skills."

After two tours with the U.S. Army, Mason found himself looking for a new adventure. A recreational diver, he decided to attend the Divers Academy of the Eastern Seaboard in Camden, New Jersey After logging more than 720 hours of classroom and underwater training in the 20-week program, Mason found a job based in the metro-Detroit area. It's not uncommon, however, to find him working all around Michigan and Ohio, with occasional jobs in other parts of the country.

In addition to the challenges and variety, Mason also appreciates the closeness that often develops between fellow employees. These friendships not only help to create a pleasant atmosphere in which to work, but they're essential because the life of each diver depends on the other members of the dive team.

"When recreational scuba divers ask about my job," Mason says, "I tell them, 'Do it! You'll enjoy it.'"

as much as 16 hours a day, seven days a week.

Working primarily in warmer climates, offshore divers are much more likely than inland divers to work year-round. But, just like inland divers, offshore workers experience periods of time when they don't dive due to work slowdowns.

Before diving in, of course, you need to hit the books. There are several schools around the country that offer courses and/or programs in commercial diving, although there are no national certification standards for commercial dive schools or programs. However, several schools are accredited by the Association of Commercial Diver Educators (ACDE). ACDE-accredited schools have at least 25 years of experience training commercial divers, and they follow training guidelines and standards approved by the American National Standards Institute (ANSI).

At dive school, you'll learn how to inspect boats, barges, docks, bridges, and other underwater structures. You'll study first aid and CPR, dive physics, underwater

psychology, decompression, rigging, salvage, demolition, and underwater photography. You'll learn various diving techniques, and you'll discuss other dive-related topics. Specific classes will depend on the school or program that you choose.

Other commercial divers get their training in a U.S. Navy diver training program. After their commitment to the military is complete, these Navy divers take their skills to a job in the private sector.

Once you've been trained, you'll start as a *tender*—the diver who stays above water, monitoring the job. He or she communicates with the divers; tracks and logs divers' depths, air consumption, and time under water; and operates the air compressors. Eventually, after getting lots of on-the-job experience, the tender can start diving. The amount of time spent as a tender varies from company to company, but inland divers spend less time working as tenders than do offshore divers.

If you've had plenty of experience and your skills are top-notch, you might decide to become a *saturation diver*. These divers work deep underwater, sometimes for longs periods of time. Because of the skills required and the added dangers they face, saturation divers usually earn the most money.

Once you've developed strong trade skills and established a long record of safe diving, you might decide to become a dive supervisor or project manager. Eventually you could become a commercial diving instructor, or even open your own dive company.

Pitfalls

Commercial divers face a high risk of on-the-job injury. One of the most serious problems commercial divers face is decompression sickness (also known as *the bends*), which can be quite painful and occasionally fatal. It also can lead to blindness and paralysis. Commercial diving is very physically and mentally demanding, which is why 90 percent of commercial divers eventually change careers. Many commercial diving jobs are seasonal.

Perks

For people who love recreational scuba diving and are interested in working in general construction, a career in commercial diving offers the best of both worlds.

Get a Jump on the Job

Commercial divers need strong swimming skills, so it's important to train. If you've never had an opportunity to scuba dive, take a class and make sure that you like it enough to do it every day.

COOK IN ANTARCTICA

OVERVIEW

Slinging hash at a remote scientific station in Antarctica might not be everybody's idea of a dream job, but for some adventure lovers, living and working at the South Pole is worth the challenge. A cook in Antarctica is expected to turn out great food under stressful conditions using some *really* unusual ingredients—like dehydrated cottage cheese and frozen dairy products. After all, if you run out of paprika at McMurdo Station, you can't just trot over to your local convenience store for more.

This is why being "adaptable" is so important to prospective cooks in Antarctica. Raytheon Polar Services—the company that does the hiring for support personnel in Antarctica—say they want people willing to invest their talents, time, and energy to ensure the success of the National Science Foundation's U.S. Antarctic Program. Applicants can expect to be grilled about their skill level and personality. A chef at the Pole must know how to cook for large groups of people and be able to create high-quality vegetarian dishes at the drop of a hat. You need to be a talented baker too, with experience whipping up cakes and cookies at high altitudes. (Altitude does make a difference when you're baking!)

You've also got to be able to deal with stress, because being a cook at the Pole is a high-stress, emotionally draining, and physically exhausting occupation. You can't fake your resume

AT A GLANCE

Salary Range

About $550 per week for 54 hours (six nine-hour days). All travel expenses are paid by Raytheon, the only company that hires for support positions at the Pole.

Education/Experience

Preferably a graduate of a culinary arts program or an apprenticeship program; minimum of three years' cooking experience, with at least one year in high-volume facilities (not including convenience or fast food).

Personal Attributes

Tolerance, ability to handle stress and very little private time, and no objections to working in close quarters with many others.

Requirements

U.S. citizenship (or permanent resident status), driver's license, and valid passport. Candidates must also pass stringent physical and dental exams, including a psychological examination for those "wintering on the ice."

Outlook

Competition is keen for these jobs, and getting a job in Antarctica will continue to be tough.

here, as you'll be put to the ultimate test once you arrive—and you'll probably be doing so under the influence of some degree of altitude sickness in that first week. Workers at the station consume more calories than you can imagine because of the high altitude and the extreme cold, and crankiness runs high. The boss demands that you remain cheerful, since the galley is like the home center on a station. Cooks in Antarctica also must be prepared to work longer than a 54-hour workweek (six- or seven-

Stephanie Rowatt, former cook in Antarctica

I've had very strong emotional ties and an instinctive pull toward anything polar that could not be ignored," says Stephanie Rowatt about her four-month stint as cook in Antarctica. But it took her three years of applying before she finally got the job. She recalls that her application process was grueling, including extensive phone interviews involving her responses to hypothetical scenarios. But she endured the long interview process because she was fascinated with Antarctica. "I despise heat, and love extreme cold. I love remoteness and personal challenge. I didn't particularly want the job as cook, but that is the area in which I had the most previous experience."

Stephanie discovered that she'd have to work harder and longer than she have imagined. "Be prepared for being more tired and living under spartan but adequate conditions. Be prepared for high altitude ...and extreme cold. You must remain cheerful, no matter what. But it was worth every minute to be able to live in such a wild and beautiful place."

day workweeks are typical)—at one of the most demanding jobs on a station. You should expect to live in dormitory-style rooms with roommates and shared bathroom facilities.

As a contract employee, a cook at an Antarctic station works for as long as the contract stipulates: either for the "summer season" (from October to February) or for the "summer/winter season" (October to October). You must leave after that. Once your contract is up, you must go through the hiring process all over again if you want to hire on for another season—not such an easy task considering that positions in Antarctica are highly competitive. About 300 people apply for every opening at McMurdo Station.

You'll find that the diverse back-grounds, skills, and interests of the workforce add to the overall experience of working and living on this beautiful continent. Each research station is its own small community with an interesting variety of activities, including hiking and cross-country skiing, crafts, sports, exercise equipment, libraries, movies, educational classes, and science lectures. Each station also operates a small general store that stocks personal articles and souvenirs. Finally, you can expect a well-balanced, comprehensive pay and benefits package, generous recognition and incentive plans, and innovative quality-of-life programs.

Pitfalls

It can be stressful in Antarctica. Being a cook at the Pole is an emotionally draining and physically tiring job. As soon as you get off the plane you'll have to start cooking—probably while under the influence of altitude sickness the first week. Because workers at the station often get a little cranky because of the high altitude, cramped conditions, and the extreme cold, the boss demands that cooks remain cheerful—so the other Antarctica workers can relax and think of the kitchen as a second home. Moreover, you can't simply quit if you don't like it, or stay on indefinitely if you do. If you're a cook in Antarctica, you'll work nine hours a day, six or seven days a week. Privacy is a premium, since you share dormitory-style rooms and cramped bathroom facilities.

Perks

Despite the cold and cramped conditions, the job can be a lot of fun. The other people who work at the Pole have a wide range of backgrounds, skills, and interests. Each research station is its own small community: On your free time, you could hike and cross-country ski, do crafts, participate in sports, work out on exercise equipment, go to the library or the movies, or take classes or science lectures. You might not be able to go to the mall, but at least you could visit a small general store on the station that stocks personal articles and souvenirs. Cooks can expect a nice salary and benefits—not to mention the once-in-a-lifetime experience of living at the end of the Earth.

Get a Jump on the Job

If you want to snag a job as cook in Antarctica, you'll need lots of cooking experience—so start now! Cook at home, take cooking courses at school, and think about applying to a culinary arts program. For a summer or after-school job, see if you can get a job as an apprentice chef, sous-chef, or even salad chef at a local restaurant. Even small places can give you some great cooking experience.

CORONER

OVERVIEW

Day or night, whenever or wherever an unexplained or unexpected death takes place, someone is called in to investigate. In the United States, death investigations are handled differently in each state. In some states deaths are investigated by a state, district, or county medical examiner. In other states, a state medical examiner oversees the investigations done by county or district medical examiners or coroners. In some states, investigations are the responsibility of the district or county medical examiner or coroner. Other states have a coroner in every county or district.

The types of deaths investigated also vary from state to state. In almost all states, violent, criminal, suspicious, or un-explained deaths are always investigated. Coroners are also usually called when a body is found dead. Depending on the state, coroners might investigate the reasons for other deaths as well. They might look into the sudden death of a person who was in good health, or they might investigate if the death appears to be a suicide. Some states ask that accidental deaths be investigated, including drowning and motor vehicle accidents. If a child dies, coroners may be called in to find the cause.

To figure out the cause of death, the coroner will collect evidence at the scene of the death, interview anyone who might have witnessed the death, and review the dead person's medical history and records. Coroners sometimes have assistants who help them with the investigation. The coroner will also read through the autopsy report as part of the investigation.

After analyzing all the evidence, the coroner makes a decision about how the person died, and that cause of death will then be listed on the death certificate. The coroner may need to write a report explaining the cause of death, and how it was determined. If the person died as the result of a crime, the coroner may have to testify at a hearing or trial.

Not surprisingly, the requirements to become a coroner vary from state to state. In some states, the requirements are left up to the district or county. Coroners are usually appointed or elected. In some places, qualifications only specify that the person be 18 years old and a resident of the county or district he or she serves.

P. Michael Murphy, coroner

With almost 13,000 deaths in Clark County, Nevada, each year, it's hard to imagine that the coroner's office would ever have an average day. But occasionally, "there is that average day when everything is running according to schedule and appropriately, while rare," says P. Michael Murphy, Clark County coroner.

Clark's background is in law enforcement, and he received his training during his 30 years on the job—plus having some advanced education. He notes that experience and training comes into play on almost every case. "Some of the forensic challenges that are placed on us require some unique skills and forward thinking," he says, "not accepting the status quo and understanding the need to think outside the box."

For Murphy, one of the things he likes most about his job is the ability to interact with and help families at their time of crisis. He takes seriously the responsibility of speaking for the people who died, and telling the truth about their situation. "But the actual time that it requires to do the job and do it effectively and appropriately," he adds, "has always put a strain on personal life and the ability to balance both.

A medical background or at least a background in anatomy would be helpful, Murphy believes, and the investigative experience he got while working as a police officer was important. "For this particular job," he says, "you'd need an administrative background to run the office itself. Gain as much experience as possible, get the education early on, and associate yourself with an office either in a volunteer status or in some type of intern status so that you can gain the insight and knowledge that you need to make sure that this is the type of career that you want. Then begin the process of working your way through the system."

In other places, the coroner must be a medical doctor to be appointed or elected.

If you're interested in being a coroner someday, there may be few or no requirements for you to run for election or to be appointed to a coroner position—but in reality you really need a very strong background in many different areas. Knowledge of law enforcement or criminal justice will help you collect and analyze the evidence. A medical background or coursework will help you read and analyze medical records and autopsy reports. College classes in criminal justice, forensics, anatomy, biology, pharmacology, fire science, nursing, management, and business administration will help give you good background. Some

colleges and universities even offer a degree in death investigation. As you sort through evidence to try to find a cause of death, a broad knowledge encompassing a lot of different areas will be a big help.

After you're appointed or elected, you might be required to complete a training class, and you'll probably be required to go to training each year to learn new information and techniques while keeping your skills up to date.

Pitfalls

Coroners are on call 24 hours a day, seven days a week. They are called to death scenes on holidays, on weekends, and in the middle of the night. In many areas, coroners make less than other elected officials (such as managers and treasurers) who put in 40 hours a week, Monday through Friday.

Perks

You'll be able to give a family answers about how their loved one died. That can be important for a family in a time of grief.

Get a Jump on the Job

Find out what the requirements are for death investigators in your area, or in the area in which you'd like to work, and work towards meeting those requirements. If there are no requirements, work toward taking college courses in criminal justice and pre-medicine, along with a variety of other classes to give you a broad background. Some coroner's offices have volunteer opportunities. Sometimes these volunteers get to help the coroner with death investigations. Check to see what kinds of hands-on opportunities are available in your area.

CRIME SCENE CLEANUP TECHNICIAN

OVERVIEW

Each week, millions of TV viewers tune in to watch their favorite crime scene investigators and detectives pop evidence into little plastic bags at the crime scene. What they don't show on TV is what happens after the investigators return to their labs and the detectives head out to catch the criminals. In the real world, when the investigators and detectives leave, someone is usually left with a big (and sometimes really awful) mess. More and more, that someone is a crime scene cleanup technician, sometimes called a *bio-recovery technician*.

Crime scene cleanup experts are often called in to clean up blood, body fluids, and body tissue after a suicide, murder, or natural death. But that's not the only thing that crime scene or bio-recovery technicians do. Sometimes they're hired to clean cars after accidents so they can be resold or stripped for parts. They're also the ones who clean up methamphetamine labs, decontaminate buildings after an anthrax exposure, or deal with rodent infestations. They're even hired to clean up the messy fingerprint dust used by the investigators and detectives.

Depending on the situation, crime scene cleanup companies may be hired by the victim, surviving family members, businesses, insurance companies—or even the police departments, who use cleanup companies to disinfect police cars.

AT A GLANCE

Salary Range

$15 to $45 per hour.

Education/Experience

None required, but a high school diploma or a GED may help.

Personal Attributes

You should be mature, physically fit, independent, and able to work under unpleasant or downright gruesome conditions. Being able to separate yourself from what you're doing at your job helps.

Requirements

None.

Outlook

Since the first crime scene cleanup business opened in Maryland in 1993, there has been rapid growth in this field. That growth is expected to continue.

Insurance companies usually pick up the tab.

In addition to cleanup, disinfecting, and removal services, many crime scene cleanup experts offer restoration services. That means after the cleanup is done, they'll repair or replace any damaged flooring or drywall, priming and painting as needed.

In most cases, you don't need any prior experience or education to become a crime scene cleanup technician. Your employer will teach you how to keep yourself safe when you're working in hazardous situations—including how to wear protective gear and how to handle the hazardous materials you'll be cleaning up. You'll learn how to tidy up crime scenes and remove any unpleasant smells. You'll learn how to safely clean, remove, package,

Andrew Yurchuck, crime scene cleanup technician

Sometimes success is a matter of having the right skills at the right time. For cleaning company owner Andrew Yurchuck, those skills were a background in emergency medical services and a master's degree in business. When Yurchuck opened New Jersey-based Bio-Clean in 1997, there were 12 companies in the country doing crime scene cleanup. Today, there are more than 500.

Yurchuck admits that the term "crime scene cleanup" isn't completely accurate.

"Only 10 percent of what we do are actual crime scenes," he explains. Instead, he's called in to clean up any type of biohazardous situation, such as the time he needed to clean up a police station bathroom where a woman had given birth. The type of cleaning is typically physically demanding work, made worse by the biohazard suits workers wear. Most of Yurchuck's employees are men in their 20s and 30s, and it's not an easy job. "Do your research and apprentice with a good company," he advises. "It's hard to make it as a technician; you really need to be a hardworking owner to be successful.

"We see the worst of the worst of the worst," he says. But for Yurchuck, the reward is helping people through one of the worst experiences of their lives.

and dispose of biohazardous materials and waste. You'll also learn about the laws and regulations you need to follow to do this job safely while protecting other people and the environment.

There are Occupational Safety and Health Administration (OSHA), Environmental Protection Agency (EPA), state, and local health department rules for dealing with biohazardous materials. You'll even be trained on how to preserve the crime scene if you discover evidence that the investigators or detectives missed.

Your employer also might want you to become a certified bio-recovery technician. You can do that by completing a course offered by the American Bio-Recovery Association (ABRA) and scoring at least 70 percent on the certification test.

Pitfalls

Crime scene cleanup technicians work in heavy, protective biohazard suits, covered from head to sweaty foot for long periods of time. You may be on call 24 hours a day, seven days a week, including weekends and holidays, but employment may be part time depending on the needs in your area.

Perks

As a crime scene cleanup technician, you'll be helping the event's survivors during one of the worst experiences of their lives.

Get a Jump on the Job

Since as much as one third of the job involves demolition and reconstruction, you might consider getting some experience painting, or replacing flooring and windows. Experience or certification in fire, mold, or flood restoration will give you an advantage when looking for a job. Preference may also be given to applicants who already have their bio-recovery technician certificate.

CYBERSLEUTH

OVERVIEW

From identity theft to child pornography and counterfeit prescription drugs, the Internet has become the new Wild West for the criminal element. But it's also developed into a major business opportunity for computer-savvy cybersleuths. The number of security companies that patrol the shady corners of this virtual world of bits and bytes is small—but growing. For example, ICG, a Princeton, New Jersey, company founded in 1997, has grown from eight employees and $1.5 million in revenue four years ago to 35 employees and a $7 million income this year. ICG, which is licensed as a private investigator in New Jersey, tracks down online troublemakers for major corporations around the world, aiming at spammers and disgruntled former employees as well as scam artists, using both technology and more traditional cat-and-mouse tactics.

For example, online identity theft alone cost businesses and consumers more than $5 billion worldwide in 2003, while spamming drained $3.5 billion from corporate coffers. In 2003, 215,000 cases of identity theft were reported to the Federal Trade Commission, an increase of 33 percent from the year before. And those numbers are climbing. The main problem is that the Internet was never designed to be secure.

There are basically two types of cybersleuths: people who hunt down people's identities (such as sleuths who help cops catch pedophiles) and those who do forensic work, looking for evidence stored on a criminal's computers and computer media.

AT A GLANCE

Salary Range

$55,000 to $100,000+

Education/Experience

More and more colleges are offering computer forensics courses; a college degree and basic experience with computers (especially Windows or NT operating systems) is important.

Personal Attributes

Curiosity, patience, attention to detail, excellent communication skills, articulate, ability to serve as expert witness, and good teaching skills.

Requirements

The University of Washington offers a certification program for computer forensics experts; there are no licensure requirements for computer forensics specialists.

Outlook

The career opportunities are booming for computer experts, and will only increase as computer technology becomes more complex.

Who hires cybersleuths? Just about anybody who needs to pry information out of a criminal's hard drive. This might include drug companies, lawyers, banks, Internet service providers, digital entertainment groups, and telecommunication giants. For example, when a spam problem crippled a Swedish telecommunications company with unwanted phone sex ads, cybersleuths plugged the spam message into search engines and tracked down other places on the Web where the message appeared. This led to some e-mail addresses, which led to a defunct e-fax Web site, which had in its registry the name of the spammer—a middle-aged man living in

Joan Feldman, cybersleuth

I just love my job," says Joan Feldman, founder and president of Computer Forensics, Inc., of Seattle, Washington. "Every time technology changes, there's something new to learn. I don't want to do the same thing every day."

The chance of *that* happening is minute, since the shadowy world of cybercriminals guarantees that somebody will be up to some new illegal activity just about all the time. "You get to solve mysteries and you're challenged by the constantly changing technology," Feldman says.

Feldman has been helping to crack hard drive crime for the past 12 years. "The more you do it, the better you get," she explains. Armed with a sociology background, she started out working with legal firms, helping them do research, reviewing millions of pages of documents and designing databases to manage the material. Her experience in litigation support and computers was the perfect foundation for the new field of cybersleuthing: She started the first cybersleuthing company in the United States, and notes that "the field has grown up around me. I got to invent a lot of the rules." When she started out, she was a lone woman in a man's world of law enforcement and technology; her first and biggest cases both came from referrals from women attorneys.

"I don't rest easy until my evidence has been checked 100 times," she says. "People who are obsessive or compulsive would do great in this job!"

Washington, D.C. After a threatened lawsuit, the man agreed to a $100,000 civil settlement.

People getting into the cybersleuth game today can expect an unending supply of work—the Internet almost guarantees an unending supply of cybercriminals. Right now, most criminals are targeting the digital theft of music and movies, illegal prescription drug sales, and identity theft. Identity thieves known as *phishers* pose as representatives of financial institutions and send out fake e-mails to people asking for their account information. The Anti-Phishing Working Group estimates that 5 to 20 percent of recipients respond to these phony e-mails.

Cybersleuths who help track down evidence stored on computers work with lawyers, advising them on what to look for or what to ask. For example, in one case against a major discount department store charged with discrimination against women, cybersleuths advised attorneys to review what was on the company's servers, to make sure the company doesn't delete its e-mails, preserves its payroll information, and keeps all of their training and testing information to make sure they will be able to tell whether women scored as well as men on the tests.

Although at the moment there aren't any licensure or certification requirements, cybersleuths predict that will soon change. The University of Washington began offering a certification program in computer forensics in spring 2005. Technical colleges sometimes offer two-year programs as well. Up to about 10 years ago, the primary training ground for cybersleuths was law enforcement—specifically, the Federal Law Enforcement Training Center (FLETC), which has the best computer forensics training for federal officers (such as the FBI and the Secret Service). You can still attend the training center, but it's only open to federal officers.

Otherwise, those interested in cyber-sleuthing can attend universities now just beginning to offer computer forensics courses, or training programs offered by companies who write computer forensic software. The High Tech Crimes Investigators Association also provides training without requiring you to be in law enforcement.

Pitfalls

Cybersleuthing carries an enormous responsibility, since many cases involve tens of millions of dollars.

Perks

Cybersleuthing can be exciting—especially to those who love solving puzzles and ferreting out hidden information. Computer forensic work can take investigators to corporate offices throughout the world—sometimes in the dead of night, searching through suspects' hard drives looking for *vampire data* (old e-mails and documents that the computer users thought they had deleted long ago). The income is often excellent and the physical risk negligible.

Get a Jump on the Job

One of the best ways to prepare yourself for a cybersleuth career is to learn all you can about Windows and NT operating systems, learning how information is managed and stored on personal computers. It's also a good idea to take any courses you can (in high school or on the college level) in computer network architecture and applications, since in future most of the action will focus on the enterprise systems that companies use to host data.

DRUG ENFORCEMENT ADMINISTRATION SPECIAL AGENT

OVERVIEW

As a Drug Enforcement Administration (DEA) special agent, you'll play an important role in fighting the serious problem of drug trafficking. Your job will be to uncover criminal drug activity and to track down and catch major drug suppliers. Your work will primarily focus on large-scale operations involving illegitimate drugs such as heroin, cocaine, hallucinogens, and marijuana. You'll also investigate both legal and illegal activities involving depressants, stimulants, and other controlled substances.

In order to get the job done, you'll collect evidence and conduct investigations—questioning informants, witnesses, and suspects—and infiltrate drug-trafficking organizations. Depending on the circumstances, you might investigate possible money laundering. Once you have sufficient evidence, you'll arrest a suspect and confiscate illegal drugs. You'll often be called upon to testify in criminal court cases to help prosecutors get a conviction.

Becoming a DEA special agent is tough. Anyone interested must first meet all of the basic requirements. Applicants must also successfully complete a written and oral assessment, a medical exam, a physical task test, a polygraph exam, a psychological assessment, and an exhaustive background check.

AT A GLANCE

Salary Range

$39,899 to more than $100,000, plus overtime and benefits.

Education/Experience

A college diploma. Applicants with college training in police science, military police experience, or both should have the best opportunities.

Personal Attributes

Able to think clearly and make decisions under pressure.

Requirements

U.S. citizen between 21 and 36 years at the time of appointment with a valid driver's license. Uncorrected vision of at least 20/200, corrected vision of 20/20 in one eye and 20/40 in the other eye, with normal color vision. Disqualifications include radical keratotomy eye surgery and hearing aids. Must be able to pass a background check and obtain a Top Secret security clearance, with excellent physical condition with the ability to lift and carry 45 pounds or more.

Outlook

Employment is expected to grow faster than the average for all occupations through 2012; concern about drugs and drug-related crimes should contribute to the increasing demand for DEA services. The opportunity for public service through law enforcement work is attractive to lots of people because the job is challenging and involves personal responsibility. Also, agents may retire with a pension after 20 or 25 years of service, allowing them to pursue a second career while still in their 40s. Because of relatively attractive salaries and benefits, the number of qualified candidates often exceeds the number of job openings, which means employers can be choosy. Competition should remain keen for higher-paying jobs and police departments in more affluent areas.

William Grant, DEA special agent

Making a difference in the world is important to DEA special agent William Grant, staff coordinator with the DEA Office of Public Affairs in Arlington, Virginia. "When you've gotten drug dealers off the street, you feel like you've made a difference in the world," he explains. Interested in becoming a policeman, Grant had majored in criminal justice in college. But after working on the police force, he transferred to the U.S. Marshall service. Part of his job was transferring prisoners, so he found himself spending a lot of time in court. That's where he first saw the DEA in action; as he sat there listening to the agents testify, he realized that's where he wanted to be.

"Being a DEA special agent gives you the opportunity to travel the world, experience a lot," he says. In the course of his official duties, he's spent time in Nepal, Norway, Finland, Thailand, and Laos. And although being a DEA agent can take up a lot of your time, Grant explains, "I took this job knowing there would be a lot of hours. I don't mind putting in the time."

The only thing he's not so fond of is the paperwork—"but it's not so bad, once you figure out how to get it all done." One of Grant's favorite things about the job is the relationship and camaraderie with the other officers—not just DEA agents, but also local and state cops with whom he works closely. "You feel like family," he says, "and no matter where you go in the world, there are DEA agents to help you."

If you meet the basic requirements and are eventually offered a job, you'll head off for 16 weeks of training at the DEA Training Academy in Quantico, Virginia. While you're there, you'll study and train at the state-of-the-art facility which opened in the spring of 1999. Inside the classroom, you'll learn the basics of writing reports, working with automated information systems, recognizing drugs, and about the laws they are enforcing. Out of the classroom, you'll complete 84 hours of physical fitness and defensive tactics training. You'll also receive 120 hours of firearms training. That training includes basic marksmanship, weapons safety, tactical shooting, and deadly force decision training. The DEA and the Federal Bureau of Investigation share facilities at Quantico for physical fitness training, firearms, training, defensive driving training, and practical application exer-

cises. There is a focus on leadership, ethics, and human dignity in each topic of study.

Throughout your 16-week training period, you'll be required to put your knowledge to the test in a series of practical exercises. These exercises are designed to test your leadership, decision making, and knowledge of procedures and techniques.

To graduate, you have to maintain an average of 80 percent on your academic exams, pass the firearms qualifications test, show leadership skills and good decision making during your practical scenario exercises, and pass a rigorous physical tasks test. After graduation from the DEA Training Academy you'll be sworn in as a DEA special agent. You'll be assigned to one of the 21 division field offices located around the United States.

Graduation and an assignment don't mean that your learning is done. Drug traffickers are constantly developing new methods and techniques to distribute drugs. To stay up-to-date with the latest trends, you might attend seminars or workshops. You'll also coordinate with and learn from other law enforcement agencies. You'll also learn on the job, with each investigation and bust.

Pitfalls

DEA special agents can be assigned to any field office in the United States, which might mean relocating away from family and friends. You'll even be required to sign a statement agreeing to this before you are hired. You can be reassigned to other field offices to meet the agency's needs. As with any job in law enforcement, working as a DEA special agent is a dangerous job with a higher-than-average chance of being injured on the job.

Perks

As a DEA special agent you'll be a member of the premier federal drug law enforcement team in the world.

Get a Jump on the Job

A number of colleges offer DEA internships; check with your college to see if they offer this program. High school students who think they might want to work for the DEA should consider attending a college with a top criminal justice program, such as Northeastern University or Texas A&M.

While you're in college, try to maintain at least a 2.95 grade point average in criminal justice, police science, finance, economics, accounting, computer science/information systems, telecommunications, electrical or mechanical engineering, Spanish, Russian, Hebrew, Arabic, Nigerian, or Chinese. A large percentage of trainees arrive at the DEA Academy with law enforcement or military experience. You might consider getting some experience in one of those areas before applying for a job as a DEA special agent.

Above all, any student contemplating a DEA position should avoid all illegal drugs and try to stay out of trouble in general. The tough criminal background check will eliminate anyone with these problems.

ELECTRIC COMPANY LINEMAN

OVERVIEW

It's midnight, a major thunderstorm has knocked out power to 10,000 customers, and there's the electric company lineman, shimmying up that utility pole with the wind lashing his coat and the rain pelting his face, trying to restore power to their customers—with lightening strikes a real possibility.

Sound like fun? That's the adventurous aspect of this job, where you're responsible for a vast network of wires and cables providing customers with electrical power and communications services. The electrical power lines deliver electricity from generating plants to customers—lines that are constructed and maintained by line installers.

Of course, not every day is as exciting as restoring power in the middle of a storm. The day-to-day work may include stringing cable along the poles, towers, tunnels, and trenches, working from a truck-mounted bucket to reach the top of the pole. Other linemen must physically climb a pole or tower. However you get there, once you're up, you pull up cable from large reels mounted on trucks and set in place, pulled tight. Then you'd attach the cable to the structure using hand and hydraulic tools.

When working with electrical power lines, installers bolt or clamp insulators onto the poles before attaching the cable. Because of the danger of electrocution with

AT A GLANCE

Salary Range

$13.22 to $32.08 an hour.

Education/Experience

A high school diploma is required. Line installers and repairers are trained on the job, and require a technical knowledge of electricity and electronics, and experience at vocational/technical programs, community colleges, or the Armed Forces. A basic knowledge of algebra and trigonometry, and mechanical ability is also helpful. More advanced supervisory positions often require a college diploma.

Personal Attributes

Customer service and interpersonal skills are important. Because the work entails lifting heavy objects (many employers require applicants to be able to lift at least 50 pounds), climbing, and other physical activity, applicants should be strong, coordinated, and not afraid of heights. The ability to distinguish colors is necessary because wires and cables may be color-coded.

Requirements

Government safety regulations strictly define the training and education requirements for apprentice electrical line installers.

Outlook

Little or no growth in employment of electrical power line installers and repairers is expected through 2012. Although the demand for electricity is rising, industry deregulation is pushing companies to lower costs, which cuts jobs; opportunities are best for workers with experience and training.

high-voltage power lines, line installers must use electrically insulated protective devices and tools when working with live cables. Underground cable is laid directly in a trench, pulled through a tunnel, or strung through a conduit running through a trench.

John Stehman, electric company operations supervisor

Ever since he watched the electric company linemen working on the power lines near his house as a boy, John Stehman dreamed of being a lineman. "I was intrigued," he recalls, "watching the lineman climb the poles, working outside. And my neighbor was a lineman too."

After graduation and an unsatisfying indoor job with a local corporation in research and development, he realized that a desk job was definitely not what he wanted to do for the rest of his life. When he found out his local electric company, PPL, was hiring, he signed on for the basic three-year, in-house training (today, it's a five-year process).

"I was blessed to have chosen a profession that I really enjoyed," he says today. He particularly enjoyed working with customers installing new lines, and—as in all construction jobs—the enormous satisfaction of creating something that didn't exist before. During his years on the job, he installed new lines, handled repairs, and—the most exciting part of the job—went out in the worst of storms to restore power.

That was the only part of the job that was a challenge, he notes. "Working on hot days, cold, icy, windy days—the changing extremes of weather could be difficult." So, too, was the knowledge that being a lineman is a tough, risky profession. "The biggest hazard is working with such high voltages," he says. "Not all jobs are right along smooth roads, not all jobs use a bucket truck." He was injured twice, once during a fall and once with "flashed eyes" from an electric flash. "It's a tough, demanding job," he says, "but it can be very fulfilling."

You also might set up service for customers, stringing cable between the customer's house and the outside electric lines, installing wiring to houses, and checking connections for proper voltage readings. Or you might install and replace transformers, circuit breakers, switches, fuses, and other equipment to control and direct the electrical current.

Line installers also are responsible for maintaining electrical, telecommunications, and cable TV lines, traveling in trucks, helicopters, and airplanes to visually inspect the wires and cables. Sensitive monitoring equipment can automatically detect malfunctions on the network, such as loss of current flow. Once a problem has been identified, you'd travel to the location of the malfunction and repair or replace defective cables or equipment.

Many communications networks now use fiber optic cables instead of conventional wire or metal cables. Fiber optic cables are made of hair-thin strands of glass, which convey pulses of light. These cables can carry much more information at higher speeds than can conventional cables. The higher transmission capacity of fiber optic cable has allowed communication networks to offer upgraded services, such as high-speed Internet access.

If you're interested in being an electric lineman, you'll need to complete a formal apprenticeship or employer training program, which is sometimes administered jointly by the electric company and the workers' union. Apprenticeship programs last up to five years and combine formal instruction with on the job training.

When you start on this job, however, as a newbie you will probably start out working as a ground helper or tree trimmer, clearing branches from power lines. If you're good at this, you can advance to a position stringing cable and performing service installations. Eventually, with experience you can move into more sophisticated maintenance and repair positions responsible for increasingly larger portions of the network.

Many community or technical colleges offer programs in telecommunications, electronics, and/or electricity; some schools, working with local companies, offer one-year certificate programs that emphasize hands-on fieldwork; graduates get preferential hiring treatment. More advanced two-year associate degree programs provide students with a broader knowledge of telecommunications and electrical utilities technology.

Pitfalls

Working high off the ground near high-power electric lines, often during storms, can be scary and dangerous. Power lines are typically higher than telephone and cable television lines, increasing the risk of severe injury due to falls. Line installers encounter serious hazards on their jobs and must follow safety procedures. When severe weather damages electrical and communi-cations lines, line installers may work long and irregular hours to restore service.

Perks

Earnings are higher than in most other occupations that don't require postsecon-dary education. Some linemen enjoy the excitement and risks inherent in restoring power during a storm, knowing they are providing a vital service to their community.

Get a Jump on the Job

If you want to work as a lineman for the electric company, you'll need to start with a basic knowledge of algebra and trigonometry—so start polishing up on those math courses at school! If your school offers any vocational training in mechanical trades or electronics, consider signing up for those too.

Working for the electric company is also a very physical job, so you'll need to be in good shape for this career. Spend time lifting weights and working out, plus building up your endurance and stamina.

For more details about employment opportunities, contact the electrical power companies in your community.

EMERGENCY MEDICAL TECHNICIAN

OVERVIEW

You've seen them on TV—the ambulance screeches to a halt at the emergency room and out jumps a couple of uniformed medical experts. Those are the emergency medical technicians (EMTs), and their job can be plenty exciting. If you're fascinated by medicine, you don't mind needles or blood, and you have a real desire to help people—but not to spend eight years or more in medical school—then a job as an EMT might be right for you.

If you answer the call to become an EMT, you might find yourself getting called out to help with auto accidents, heart attacks, drownings, childbirth, or gunshot wounds, as you provide care as you transport the sick or injured to a medical facility.

In an emergency, a 911 operator would send you to the scene. Once you arrive at the scene, you'd determine the patient's condition; following strict guidelines, you'd give appropriate emergency care and, when necessary, transport the patient to the hospital. Emergency treatment for more complicated problems is carried out under the direction of medical doctors by radio preceding or during transport.

Usually one EMT drives while the other monitors the patient's vital signs. Some EMTs work as part of the flight crew of helicopters that transport critically ill or injured patients to hospital trauma centers.

At the hospital, EMTs help transfer patients to the emergency department, report their observations and actions to emergency room staff, and may provide more emergency treatment. After each run, you'd replace used supplies and check equipment.

The specific responsibilities of EMTs depend on their level of qualification and training. The National Registry of Emergency Medical Technicians (NREMT) registers emergency medical service (EMS) providers at four levels: First Responder, EMT-Basic, EMT-Intermediate, and EMT-Paramedic. Of course, some states have their own certification and use numeric ratings from 1 to 4 to distinguish levels of proficiency.

First responders are the lowest-level workers, who are trained to provide basic emergency medical care because they tend to be the first persons to arrive at the scene of an incident. Many firefighters, police officers, and other emergency workers have this level of training.

An EMT-Basic, also known as an EMT-1 or EMT-B, represents the first component of the emergency medical technician system. An EMT-1 is trained to care for patients at the scene of an accident and while transporting patients by ambulance to the hospital under medical direction. The EMT-1 has the emergency skills to assess a patient's condition and care for breathing, heart, and trauma emergencies.

An EMT-Intermediate, also known as an EMT-2 and EMT-3, has more advanced training that allows the EMT to administer IV fluids, use manual defibrillators to give lifesaving shocks to a stopped heart, and apply advanced airway techniques and equipment to help patients experiencing respiratory emergencies.

An EMT-Paramedic, also called an EMT-4, provides the most extensive pre-hospital care. In addition to carrying out the procedures already described, paramedics may administer drugs orally and intravenously, interpret electrocardiograms (EKGs), perform endotracheal intubations, and use monitors and other complex equipment.

While you don't need to go to college to become an EMT, you will need to be certified. All 50 states have some type of certification procedure; most require National Registry of EMT (NREMT) registration for some or all levels of certification. Other states administer their own certification examination or

provide the option of taking the NREMT examination.

To maintain certification, EMTs must reregister, usually every two years. In order to reregister, an individual must be working as an EMT and meet a continuing education requirement.

Training is offered at progressive levels: EMT-Basic (EMT-1) coursework typically emphasizes emergency skills, such as managing respiratory, trauma, and cardiac emergencies, and patient assessment. Formal courses are often combined with time in an emergency room or ambulance. The program also provides instruction and practice in dealing with bleeding, fractures, airway obstruction, cardiac arrest, and emergency childbirth. Students learn how to use and maintain common emergency equipment, such as backboards, suction devices, splints, oxygen delivery systems, and stretchers. Graduates of approved EMT basic training programs who pass a written and practical examination administered by the state certifying agency or the NREMT earn the title *Registered EMT-Basic*.

The course is a prerequisite for EMT-Intermediate (EMT-2 and EMT-3) and EMT-Paramedic (EMT-4) training. EMT-Intermediate training requirements vary from state to state. Applicants can choose to receive training in EMT-Shock Trauma, where the EMT learns to start IV fluids and give certain medications, or in EMT-Cardiac, which includes learning heart rhythms and administering advanced medications. Training commonly includes 35 to 55 hours of additional instruction beyond EMT-Basic coursework, and covers patient assessment as well as the use of advanced airway devices and intravenous fluids. Prerequisites for taking the EMT-Intermediate examination include

Heather Albright, emergency medical technician

At the age of just 16, Heather Albright of Broomall, Pennsylvania, already knew she wanted to become an EMT. Her reason was quite simple: "I wanted to help people," she says. "I really like interacting with the patients."

After joining her local ambulance corps, she began studying for the first level of EMT (EMT-Basic, or EMT-B). By age 18, Albright was driving the ambulance as an EMT-B for an ambulance company, Alternative Transport, in Prospect Park, Pennsylvania.

She loves her work, and says that being a female EMT doesn't cause her any problems at all. Long gone are the days when a woman on the crew invited hazing and hostility. These days, the only problem for women that Albright sees these days is not emotional or mental, but physical—it can be strenuous to lift and carry patients all day long.

Albright recommends that aspiring young EMTs should go beyond book learning to get some real life experience: She recommends that in addition to attending class to prepare for the EMT certification exam, you should join a fire company as an EMT volunteer so you can get firsthand, on-the-job experience.

Albright continues to work as an EMT while attending college at Penn State University and contemplating a career as a nurse. Her EMT training, she figures, provides a great background for a nursing career as well.

registration as an EMT-Basic, required classroom work, and a specified amount of clinical experience.

The most advanced level of training for this occupation is EMT-Paramedic. At this level, the EMT receives extra training in body function and learns more advanced skills. The technology program usually lasts up to two years and awards an associate degree in applied science. Such education prepares the graduate to take the NREMT examination and become certified as an EMT-Paramedic. Extensive related coursework and clinical and field experience is required.

Due to the longer training requirement, almost all EMT-Paramedics are in paid positions, rather than being volunteers. Refresher courses and continuing education are available for EMTs at all levels.

Opportunities for EMTs are expected to grow as the baby boomer generation ages and requires more emergency care. You'll find lots of jobs in private ambulance services. Competition will be greater for jobs in fire, police, and independent third-service rescue squad departments, where salaries and benefits tend to be slightly better. You'll have the best opportunities if you have an advanced certification, such as EMT-Intermediate or EMT-Paramedic.

Pitfalls

When you wake up in the morning, you never know if you're going to get a call to go out on a run where you'll confront some really serious trauma. Being an EMT can be a physically strenuous, stressful job; the hours are irregular and workers often must treat patients in life-or-death situations. Some EMTs, especially those in police and fire departments, are on call for extended periods. While it may look dramatic, exciting, and glamorous on TV, remember that EMTs also may be exposed to diseases such as hepatitis B and AIDS, as well as violence from drug overdose victims or mentally unstable patients.

Perks

Many EMTs find the work exciting and challenging. Almost all of them get into the career in the first place because they truly enjoy the opportunity to help others, and really want to give back to their community.

Get a Jump on the Job

If you're interested in an EMT career, talk to your local volunteer ambulance corps and see if you can become a member. This can give you a sense for whether you'll like the world of the EMT. Or, try an internship or volunteer position at your local hospital emergency room.

FBI SPECIAL AGENT

OVERVIEW

While you won't be spending time checking out aliens from outer space like Scully and Mulder on TV's *The X Files,* chances are you can find plenty of exciting, adventurous work in one of the divisions of the Federal Bureau of Investigation (FBI).

FBI special agents investigate a variety of crimes, including organized crime, bribery, drug trafficking, kidnapping, extortion, bank robbery, and terrorism. The FBI also works with other federal, state, and local law enforcement officers to gather evidence, interview witnesses, process information, and analyze data. Agents may be asked to track the movement of stolen property, inspect business records, perform undercover assignments, and investigate federal criminal violations.

Established in 1908, the FBI is one of the most competitive and respected law enforcement agencies in the world. The main bureau of the FBI is located in Washington, D.C., but there are lots of field offices and satellite offices located in the United States. Agents tend to gravitate to program areas where they have a personal interest or expertise: organized crime, drugs, civil rights, white-collar crime, counter-intelligence, and terrorism. In general, FBI investigations tend to be long term, involving more sophisticated techniques than the average law enforcement job. For example, agents who worked in the white-collar crime area during the 1980s found themselves investigating the savings-and-loan frauds for years.

AT A GLANCE

Salary Range

$39,115 to $85,140 (GS-10 to GS-15); overtime can add another 25 percent of your base pay per year ($48,890 to $106,430).

Education/Experience

A four-year degree from an accredited college and at least three years of full-time work experience. There are four entry programs to the FBI: Law, Accounting, Language, and Diversified. The law program requires a law degree; the accounting program requires a B.S. in accounting. The language program requires a B.S. or B.A. and fluency in a second language. The diversified program requires a B.S. or B.A. All new agents undergo 16 weeks of rigorous training at the FBI academy on the U.S. Marine Corps base in Quantico, Virginia.

Personal Attributes

Common sense goes a long way in this job; also important are determination, trustworthiness, independence, honesty, attentiveness, physical fitness, and flexibility. Good communication skills, excellent people skills, superb writing skills, strong work ethic, and the ability to function as part of a team are essential. Agents also must have good morals, sound judgment, loyalty, and the desire to fight crime and pursue justice.

Requirements

U.S. citizenship, minimum age 21 (but less than 37 at time of appointment), security clearance. Many positions require passing a polygraph exam, drug test, and color and vision tests.

Outlook

With prestige and attractive salary/benefits, competition is fierce for these jobs. The number of qualified applicants exceeds the number of openings, and the turnover rate is very low.

When you're an FBI agent, each day can be a little different depending on which program area you've chosen. You might go into the office one day and start working on solving a bank robbery, only to get an urgent call that a kidnapping just occurred. Some program areas require a lot of international travel, and some involve actually living abroad—especially in the anti-terrorism and drug-trafficking areas. Since 9/11, FBI agents are now posted in 50 embassies around the world.

If you want to be an FBI special agent, be prepared for a long process—usually about a year. First, you have to submit all sorts of forms with your application. Then, after a long wait, you take a three-part standardized test. If you pass that test, you'll face a new battery of examinations: a panel interview, a written exam, an in-depth background check, a lie detector test, and a drug test.

If you manage to thread your way through all those tests and you're still standing—you'll be accepted to *train* as an FBI agent. You'll embark on a two-year probationary period and undergo 16 weeks of training at the FBI Academy on the U.S. Marine Corps base in Quantico, Virginia—including intensive physical training, firearms training, and a wide variety of academic training.

After training, you'll be assigned to one of the FBI's field offices, where you can expect to remain for at least four years. During this time, you'll be working and guided by a veteran agent who will help you with the lessons you learned in the FBI Academy.

There's almost nothing the bad guys can do that the FBI isn't in charge of investigating: organized crime, public corruption, financial crime, fraud against the government, bribery, copyright infringement, civil rights violations, bank robbery, extortion, kidnapping, air piracy, terrorism, espionage, interstate criminal activity, drug trafficking, and other violations of federal laws. In fact, agents are the government's principal investigators, responsible for investigating violations of more than 260 laws and conducting sensitive national security investigations.

If you're lucky enough to carry the coveted FBI badge, you might conduct surveillance or monitor court-authorized wiretaps. You might need to examine business records as part of investigations of white-collar crime. Maybe you'll track the interstate movement of stolen property, collect evidence of espionage activities, or participate in sensitive undercover assignments.

Pitfalls

You must be willing to put in long hours for weeks or months doing stressful, dangerous work that often can't be fully recognized for security reasons.

Perks

There's a lot of satisfaction in catching the bad guys—terrorists, mobsters, kidnappers—and FBI agents usually get their man. Moreover, the salary for special agents is pretty good. Federal law provides special salary rates to federal employees who serve in law enforcement, and they throw in a 25 percent bonus for overtime that agents are expected to work. For example, in 2003 FBI agents entered federal service as GS-10 employees on the pay scale at a base salary of $39,115, yet earned about $48,890 a year with availability pay. They could advance to the GS-13 grade level in field nonsupervisory assignments at a base salary of $61,251, which is worth $76,560

Bill Tonkin, FBI special agent

After 29 years in the business, Special Agent Bill Tonkin says this country is facing greater challenges than ever before with the new risks of international terrorism—and the FBI is the place to be to help face those risks.

"As our world changes, our needs change," he explains. "In the 1950s, we needed Russian speakers to help fight the cold war with the KGB. Today, we need Russian speakers to help fight Russian organized crime."

Tonkin—who's assigned to the counter-terrorism detail—says he's been interested in a law enforcement career for a long time. He'd been thinking about becoming a state trooper when a friend of his at Millersville University revealed his plans about joining the FBI. Through him, Tonkin learned about how to apply.

As a special agent working against terrorism, Tonkin finds himself responding to a variety of situations, responding to incoming information from the public about potential threats, gathering information about suspicious situations from cops on the beat.

"Our job does offer personal satisfaction," Tonkin says, "whether an agent is locking up a bank robber or a bank president. Putting away the bad guys is the bottom line. There can be hardships, but ultimately there are rewards."

with availability pay. FBI supervisory, management, and executive positions at grade GS-15 payed a base salary of about $85,140 a year—or $106,430 a year with the bonus pay thrown in.

Get a Jump on the Job

Think you might be interested in becoming a G-man (or woman) someday? You can get a sample of life as an FBI agent if you're selected to participate in the FBI Honors Internship Program in Washington, D.C. The program offers college students an exciting insider's view of FBI operations and provides an opportunity to explore career opportunities. Each summer, a limited number of highly competitive internships are awarded; only highly motivated students with great grades and outstanding character are chosen. To be considered, you need to:

- be enrolled in your junior year when you apply (graduate-level students must be enrolled in a college or university and attending full time)
- be returning to your campus after the program
- have a cumulative grade point average of 3.0 or above
- be a U.S. citizen

The Honors Internship Program usually begins on the first Monday in June and ends on the second Friday in August. If you're interested in the FBI Honors Internship Program, visit the Web site (http://www.fbi.gov/employment/honors.htm) or contact the FBI field office nearest your campus for applications and additional information.

FEDERAL AIR MARSHAL

OVERVIEW

The next time you fly, that serious-looking fellow in the straw hat reading the *New York Times* could just be somebody's Uncle Frank—or he could be a federal air marshal. Unless there is a threat to the security of the plane, you'd never know which.

Most Americans had no idea there even *was* such a thing as an air marshal until September 11, 2001, when terrorists hijacked aircraft and used them as weapons. Since then, there's been much more interest in the federal air marshal program. This very special branch of law enforcement began during the 1970s, when the Sky Marshal Program was set up to help prevent hijackings to Cuba. In 1985, the Sky Marshal Program was broadened and transformed into the Federal Air Marshal Program we know today.

In the interest of national security, the information available to the public about the program is very general. Federal air marshals—also called civil aviation security specialists—have the awesome responsibility of deterring hijacking attempts and keeping passengers and crew members safe. Although the exact number of marshals isn't public knowledge, there aren't enough to cover each domestic and international flight originating in the United States. Instead, these agents fly on high-risk, secret routes worldwide, dressed like ordinary passengers so they'll blend in.

If you're hired as a federal air marshal, you'll receive special training to perform

AT A GLANCE

Salary Range

$36,000 to $84,000.

Education/Experience

Minimum of a bachelor's degree in any field, or three years' work experience.

Personal Attributes

Capable of working independently for long periods of time; able to remain calm, cool, and collected in stressful or dangerous situations.

Requirements

U.S. citizen under age 40. Physically fit with normal color vision, EKG, and hearing. Must be eligible for and able to maintain a firearm certificate and top-secret security clearance. Candidates need to show that they have specialized experience related to this line of work, such as law enforcement, security, or airline travel experience.

Outlook

The demand for federal air marshals depends on safety and security situations around the world. In general, there are far more applicants than jobs available.

your job: stopping a terrorist attack while keeping the passengers and crew as safe as possible. Training takes place both in the classroom and in practical training situations. You'll train on an outdoor shooting range, in an aircraft simulator, and on actual planes. Firearms skills are very important, so you can hit your intended target without injuring innocent bystanders. After successfully completing your training, you'll be assigned to your first mission.

As a federal air marshal, you'll be on call 24 hours a day. You won't have regular hours or shifts; instead, you'll be

> ## Note:
>
> By federal law, federal air marshals are not allowed to talk publicly about the program. Those who do can be fired and/or prosecuted. Therefore, there is no interview with a federal air marshal.

called in to work whenever and wherever you're needed. Since agents are generally assigned to high-risk flights, you'll often travel to foreign countries with political or economic problems. Some of these areas also have unsafe water, poor sanitary conditions, and problems with crime or terrorism. When you're working, you may be gone for several weeks at a time. During that time, you'll have limited contact with your family and little time off.

For all these reasons, being a federal air marshal is a very stressful job. You've got to be unflappable under pressure. Federal air marshals need to be in excellent physical shape, and you'll be required to pass an annual physical. To keep your skills sharp, you'll receive recurrent training and recertification.

Pitfalls

Every time you go to work, you'll face the possibility of being in a life-threatening situation or visiting a dangerous place. There's a lot of stress in this job.

Perks

Federal air marshals are in a position to save the lives of hundred or thousands of innocent people. That can give you a mighty good feeling of accomplishment. You'll also have the opportunity to travel all around the world while you're doing your job.

Get a Jump on the Job

If riding shotgun on a superjet is your dream and you are aiming for a job as a federal air marshal, stay in school, become familiar with the law enforcement skills and technology of the 21st century, and build a solid record of service.

FISHING GUIDE

OVERVIEW

Picture this: You're floating down a lazy winding river, the steep sides of the Rockies towering above you, past a bear dozing on a sun-warmed rock. For a fishing guide, this is the daily view out the "office" window. Fishing guides have found an ideal way to combine a love of fly-fishing, an enchantment with the outdoors, and a genuine interest in other fisher-folk—and get paid for it!

With modern-day disposable incomes on the rise, more and more individuals are becoming interested in combining fly-fishing and tourism. They depend on fishing guides to handle their travel arrangements, provide information, show points of interest, and lead them through unmarked or remote areas. Fishing guides plan, organize, and conduct fishing trips (sometimes combining them with birding trips or other outdoor adventures). They apply their knowledge of the rivers, lakes, and oceans to plan the itinerary and to determine the best route and sites.

But the job of a fishing guide involves much more than knowing how to trail a line in the water. The job often includes arranging for transportation of clients, equipment, and supplies, using horses, land vehicles, motorboats, or airplanes. If clients are inexperienced, the guide can act as fishing coach and instructor, showing how to use the equipment and explaining the area fishing laws. Many fishing guides must become amateur environmental scientists, studying the fishes' habits and habitats, the fish

themselves, the environment, and what is affecting the fish.

It's an independent life, but as with all jobs in the outdoors, it's not always easy. Guides usually work outdoors in all types of weather, rowing for long periods of time while being alert at all times to ensure the safety of the tourists and see that they are enjoying themselves. They may have to carry heavy backpacks, cook meals over open campfires, and sleep on the ground.

AT A GLANCE

Salary Range

Between $180 and $225 a day, plus tips.

Education/Experience

No formal education is necessary, but extensive fishing experience is required. College classes in biology and geography may help; most employers provide training.

Personal Attributes

Should be outgoing, friendly, gregarious, sensitive, teaching ability, and have a good sense of humor.

Requirements

In addition to fishing licenses, most states have separate license requirements for commercial guides who will be leading trips on federal waters. Separate licenses and permissions are required for guiding in foreign countries.

Outlook

With rising incomes, more people are expected to go on more frequent vacations, so fishing guide jobs are expected to increase, especially as the sport becomes more popular and different species are targeted for fly-fishing. However, the travel industry is sensitive to economic downturns, when travel plans are likely to be deferred, so the number of job opportunities can fluctuate.

Patty Reilly, fishing guide

For fishing guide Patty Reilly, her job is all about "doing what you love to do in wonderful places with a rod in your hand." A veteran professional fly-fishing guide for 23 years, Reilly lives in Jackson Hole, Wyoming, but has spent years guiding and exploring Patagonia and the Rocky Mountains. Today she runs "Guided Connections," which coordinates customized trips for fly-fishing and bird-watching as well as other outdoor adventures, such as hiking and horseback trips.

Patty began her working life as a restaurateur, and fished as a hobby. She fell in love with the rivers, trout fishing, and the scenery and wildlife of Patagonia and the Rockies, and eventually, friends began asking her to serve as their guide. "I never thought of it as a career before," she says, "but once I started guiding my friends, I thought: 'Isn't this a great way to make a living!'"

Most people who hire a guide for a river already are excellent fishermen, but don't want to have to learn a new river if they are fishing on vacation—that's where fishing guides come in.

"I've met wonderful people doing this," Reilly says, "and working in the outdoors is a wonderful way of life. The whole objective is to enjoy the environment, the birds, the animals you encounter—and if you get a fish too, that's great. Many days, you don't get a fish. You can't ever really perfect it."

Pitfalls

The job can be physically demanding, especially for float-fishing guides on rivers in western states, who must row the boats for their clients. Guides also must deal with all types of people, which can sometimes be difficult.

Perks

Being able to earn a very good living while working in the outdoors and participating in a favorite sport captures the interest of sportfishing experts who decide to become fishing guides. Most guides also enjoy the travel, the independent aspect of the job, plus sharing what they love with others who have similar interests.

Get a Jump on the Job

If you dream of becoming a fishing guide, odds are you're probably already an avid fisherman. Build up your resume now with lots of experience with your rod and reel. Handling a boat is also often important, depending on the type of fishing you're doing, so lots of practice in boating will also come in handy.

You might consider signing up for teen white-water camps. NOVA, Alaska's oldest adventure travel company, offers teen programs (http://www.nova-alaska.com).

GRAND CANYON HELICOPTER PILOT

OVERVIEW

While lots of folks prefer to ride on a mule to the bottom of the Grand Canyon, the elderly and people with disabilities don't have that option—and that's where the Grand Canyon helicopter pilots come in. Taking tourists on a quick trip to see the wonders of the Grand Canyon is all in a day's work for these helicopter pilots, many of whom are Vietnam vets.

Although the various tour companies offer slightly different tours, taking off from different points along the Canyon, the basic job of piloting this complex craft remains the same. In general, the helicopter flight isn't just an elevator ride to the floor of one of the nation's biggest tourist attractions—it's a hair-raising weave through the walls of the Grand Canyon itself. During the ride, many younger pilots rely on prerecorded narration about generic sights along the Canyon. Older, more experienced pilots like to do their own narration—unless foreign visitors require language tapes because they don't speak English.

Most pilots at the Grand Canyon work a seven-days-on, seven-days-off shift. Other part-timers work every other week, or just weekends through the summer.

If you have a hankering to pilot one of those big boys, you'll need to get a private pilot's certificate with a helicopter rating, and then you'll need to earn a commercial

certificate with a helicopter rating. You can get a private pilot's certificate at 17; with that piece of paper, you'll need more training and more flight time to work up to your commercial license. You'll do a minimum of 150 hours of flight time and 30 hours of ground instruction, and then have to pass a written exam with a minimum grade of 70 percent. After passing the written test, next comes an oral and a flight test.

Pitfalls

While today's helicopters are very safe, that still doesn't mean they're easy to fly, no matter where you're going. And the

Don Clarke, Grand Canyon helicopter pilot

Flying is something that people fall in love with," says helicopter pilot Don Clarke of Cumru, Pennsylvania. "You have to have a healthy respect for what you're doing." Helicopter flying is far more complex than an airplane, he explains, and far more difficult to fly. Helicopter pilots must master more forces—maneuvering up, down, back and forth, and side to side.

"Basically, an airplane wants to fly," he says. "A helicopter wants to crash." Airplanes are designed for stability, so that even if the engine cuts out, an experienced pilot could theoretically glide the plane to a safe (albeit bumpy) landing. "The only thing that's stable about a helicopter," Clarke says, "is the pilot's ability."

Trained in helicopter flying during the Vietnam War, Clarke came home—along with the other 40,000 trained helicopter pilots—to find there were no jobs in his field. "Unless you were willing to go to Indonesia to work, there was a much greater supply than demand."

Retired now, Clarke commutes to the west twice a month to work on a long weekend. While he loves flying the Grand Canyon, it can be challenging. Unlike an airplane, which typically boasts two pilots plus "automatic pilot" capability, on his helicopter Clarke is it. There are no other pilots and no autopilot. "For six or seven hours a day, I'm on the controls. I can't turn them loose for a second. From the moment you start to the moment you shut down, you can't let go."

Grand Canyon is more dangerous than most locations—if you've got problems with your craft, there aren't any large flat expanses of field to touch down on. It's hard to judge distance there, and most of the terrain is rocky. Typically, the helicopter accidents in the Canyon have been due to pilot error.

If danger isn't enough to deter you, the pay could be: These jobs aren't typically high-paying. Since there aren't any homes on the rim of the Grand Canyon, there's quite a bit of commuting to get to your job. Some pilots live a state away, and others live on the other side of the country, commuting to work one or two weekends a month. Helicopter pilots love to fly helicopters, and there aren't that many jobs out there for these well-trained experts. Grand Canyon flying also tends to

be seasonal, available only about nine or 10 months a year.

Perks

For many pilots, flying helicopters is the love of their lives—and it's hard to imagine a more beautiful place to fly than the Grand Canyon. Being paid to do what you love, in a phenomenally lovely location, is a mighty big perk. If you like people, it can be fun to meet tourists from all over the world who flock to these areas.

Get a Jump on the Job

At 17 you can start training for a helicopter license. Experts suggest you work hard in school and get good grades, and go on to college. The military remains the most common way to train for helicopter pilot jobs, but you can get civilian training too.

HELICOPTER TRAFFIC REPORTER

OVERVIEW

You're riding down the highway when suddenly a wall of red lights appears in front of you. Like dominoes, one set of brake lights ignites two more as you realize there must be an accident up ahead, or construction. Within seconds, the road looks like a parking lot, while more and more vehicles pour into already overcrowded streets. You sit and wait as the minutes pass, slowly inching ahead yard by yard. What's going on? What do you do?

Most likely, you switch to the local news station to find out what's causing the holdup. Each weekday morning and evening, your local traffic reporter supplies listeners with the traffic report. In fact, studies show that traffic reports are among the most listened-to programming. Especially in big cities with major potential road clogs, the radio helicopter traffic reporter is required listening for every commuter.

No one is sure when helicopter traffic reporting began, and no association even knows just how many helicopter traffic reporters there are across the nation. But in modern-day urban sprawl, the traffic spotter can see the big picture—and report back to the captive audience trapped in their cars. Typically, helicopter traffic reporters provide information on roadway conditions, feeding reports about accidents,

AT A GLANCE

Salary Range

$25,000 to $100,000+

Education/Experience

A college degree (preferably in communications or journalism) and solid knowledge of the area's geography and roadways.

Personal Attributes

Ability to work well under pressure, good communication skills, articulate.

Requirements

Knowledge of geography and roadways in reporting area and able to handle high pressure. Pilot-reporters must have a helicopter license.

Outlook

Helicopter traffic reporting jobs are difficult to find; consolidation within the industry means there aren't many openings and competition for them is fierce.

drive times, alternate route suggestions, construction and event delays, and lane and road closings to motorists listening on their radios.

Traffic-watch helicopters will normally fly on a set schedule during the morning and evening rush hours, and while they are up, they may be sent to breaking news stories such as a fire or major accident. They may do live reports on the air to more than one radio and/or TV station. These pilots and cameramen fly a split schedule with time off in the middle of the day to rest, go eat, or run errands. Most helicopters are equipped with an electronics package that will consist of a gyro-stabilized camera operated by a cameraman sitting at a console in the rear seat. The helicopter

John DelGiorno, helicopter traffic reporter

When a car accident ties up traffic in the tristate area, airborne traffic reporter John DelGiorno is one of the first to provide a solution. On the job since 1994, DelGiorno flies in a single-engine Bell Long Ranger helicopter equipped with state-of-the-art video and audio equipment.

"Our job is to report major traffic issues," DelGiorno explains to *The Long Island Commuter*. "We serve our listeners and viewers better when we describe the big spots to avoid." His morning report is part of a local TV show, *Eyewitness News This Morning*, that covers Fairfield County, Connecticut, the five boroughs of New York City, central and northern New Jersey, and Long Island. DelGiorno also performs airborne traffic reports for several affiliates, including WABC-AM and WPLJ-FM.

"You've got to have a voice that the boss and the listeners like to hear," DelGiorno says. "Some traffic reporters have an informal style. I do straight reporting and don't have room to joke around."

Every morning, DelGiorno commutes 25 minutes to a heliport in Linden, New Jersey, where he climbs into the helicopter at 5:30 a.m. He's done every day at half past noon, but after the morning rush hour the crew is on standby throughout the day for traffic and breaking news.

Flying at 1,000 feet allows a safe distance between the ground underneath and the commercial jets above. But over Manhattan, for example, the pilot tries to stay at 2,000 feet in order to avoid skyscrapers and keep the noise down.

Helicopter traffic reporters won't fly if weather conditions are poor, such as when there is low visibility, lightning, snow, or sleet. Safety is always the first priority and the station is 100 percent supportive if the pilots choose not to fly because of inclement weather, regardless of what the other stations decide.

may have several more internal or external cameras to show other views, or to show the pilot or traffic reporter's face. The helicopter will be equipped with a microwave link that transmits the camera image back to the station for them to tape or put on the air live.

The helicopter may also be set up with one or more police scanners, FM radios that enable the pilot or cameraman to talk to ground units, the staff back at the station or even to fire or police units if necessary. Of course the aircraft will have the normal VHF radio(s) for air traffic control, to talk with other helicopters in the area, plus a transponder and one or more GPS receivers. A cell phone is also wired into the aircraft audio system.

Because reports are unscripted, every day is a challenge. Today's traffic reporter uses state-of-the-art technology—including mounted camera systems and strategically located fixed-position camera systems. If you were working as a traffic reporter, you'd probably track traffic data using a variety of computer-generated data, enabling you to provide live traffic reporting with updated information every 10 minutes. You also might be expected to generate maps and other graphics for traffic reports on TV, or coordinate live video with the helicopter pilot and a feedroom technician.

Pitfalls

Helicopter traffic reporting is not without danger; there were 212 civilian helicopter crashes nationwide in 2003, 37 with fatalities, a slight increase from 2002, which saw 205 crashes, 26 that were fatal, according to the Helicopter Association International.

In 1986, Jane Dornacker, a traffic reporter for WNBC Radio in New York, was killed when her helicopter crashed into the Hudson River. The pilot was critically injured. Earlier in 1986, Dornacker and another pilot escaped unharmed when a WNBC traffic helicopter crashed into the Hackensack River in New Jersey.

Perks

There's no question that broadcasting live from a helicopter is exciting; pro-viding a vital service can be satisfying and the pressure to think fast and come up with alternate routes can provide an adrenalin rush. Typically, the job also pays fairly well and offers plenty of independence—every day is different, and never boring.

Get a Jump on the Job

Since some traffic reporters have a journalism background, you can take journalism courses and work on your school paper in high school or college. If you think you might want to combine traffic reporting with piloting a helicopter, you can start work now toward your helicopter pilot's license.

HIGH-RISE WINDOW WASHER

OVERVIEW

Believe it or not, there is more to becoming a window washer than just grabbing a squeegee and clambering up a ladder. Although you don't need any experience to get started, once you get hired you'll have a lot to learn from the experienced washers on your work crew. You'll learn how to use the cleaning equipment and chemicals, and how to decide what supplies are best for each particular job. If you'll be doing high-rise work, you'll learn how to set up and use industrial access ropes and harnesses, scaffoldings, and riggings. You'll need to become familiar with the federal Occupational Safety and Health Administration (OSHA) regulations for equipment used in window cleaning. If you'll be working in California, you also need to follow the California OSHA regulations for window cleaning.

Each workday is different for high-rise window washers, who have a variety of different jobs to do while working to make customers happy. Some days you'll spend all day working on the windows of a single high-rise building, returning to that job site for several days until the job is finished. Other days, you might work closer to the ground, cleaning the windows of houses, government buildings, shops, and other small commercial buildings. Some days you might be assigned to route work,

where you work with a crew to clean the windows of several businesses owned by the same person as one job.

For safety reasons, especially when working on high-rises, window washers usually work in teams of two or more. The camaraderie employees get from working in teams also helps to promote a pleasant work environment. You'll probably work weekdays, but some specific jobs or clients may require some evening or weekend work. Many window-washing businesses offer other services such as gutter cleaning, pressure washing, or window repair or restoration services. Your specific job duties will depend on the services that your employer offers to its customers.

Ron Friman, high-rise window washer

High-rise window washing may seem scary to some people, but to Ron Friman, it's a fun, kind of romantic occupation. "I like hanging off the side of a building, flying around," he says. "It's like being a kid on a swing. It's fun!"

Friman started window cleaning as a summer job at the age of 15. After graduating from college with a degree in computer science, Friman returned to the window-cleaning business. He opened his own company looking for freedom, and today, Friman's "Expert Window Cleaning" employs a staff of 15. Just as Friman did, many window washers start as a window cleaner and work into their own business venture.

When Friman is considering applicants, one of the things he considers is how well the person handles stress—how the person would react to situations that occur while hanging off the side of a building. "Learn everything you can about safety," advises Friman, who is also a national safety instructor for the IWCA. Friman advocates training with a professional, because practical experience is better than a day or two in the classroom. "The equipment almost never fails," Friman says. "Accidents are almost always due to human error. This isn't something that you can learn by yourself. If you have an accident, there are no second chances."

Personal accomplishment is a big part of the job. "Once you become skilled, it's quite an accomplishment that you can rig and service a building," Friman says. "When you get done with a job, you look back and think, 'How did I do that?'"

After some time on the job, your employer might want you to become a certified window cleaner. This certification is offered by the International Window Cleaner Certification Institute (IWCCI). There are four levels of certification: CWC/RR for window washers specializing in ground-based route or residential operations; CWC for window washers specializing in ground-based commercial cleaning; CMC/RDS for window washers specializing in commercial window cleaning using suspended equipment operations with rope descent systems; and CWC/SS for window washers specializing in commercial window cleaning using suspended scaffold equipment operations. Window washers must pass a final exam on material related to the level of certification they want to earn. There are four different exams, one for each level. To help

prepare, workbooks are available for each level. A specific amount of on-the-job training is also required for certification. The amount of hours required and other specifics depend on the level of certification you're earning.

Certification is becoming more and more important to employers who are concerned with your safety, which is a focus of the training. Certification is also an important selling point to many current and prospective customers who want to hire a company whose cleaners are familiar with the latest supplies and techniques and can use that information to do a good, professional job.

Additional training seminars covering all aspects of window cleaning safety and equipment usage are offered by the International Window Cleaning Association (IWCA). The IWCA is a nonprofit trade association whose purpose is to raise the standards of professionalism in the window cleaning industry. They represent all areas related to the window-cleaning industry. The IWCA holds an annual convention and trade show where window washing business owners and their employees can meet with more than 60 vendors and exhibitors, and watch live demonstrations of window cleaning products. Seminars cover a variety of topics including safety, training, bidding, marketing, employee relations, and more. There are even contests, including the IWCA Speed Window Cleaning Contest. Window washers from around the world compete for a chance to be the fastest window cleaner, and maybe even set a world's record. The key to winning is cleaning as fast as possible with the fewest mistakes.

Pitfalls

Depending on your area, window-cleaning jobs may be seasonal or part time. Window washers may suffer from bursitis, elbow pain, shoulder pain, or other repetitive motion injuries. If you specialize in high-rise work, there is a chance you could be injured on the job.

Perks

After a few years working for someone else, you might decide you'd like to be your own boss. It is relatively easy and inexpensive to get started in your own window washing business.

Get a Jump on the Job

If you plan to do high-rise work, consider checking out a rappelling clinic or similar opportunities to make sure that working at heights won't be a problem for you.

HOT-AIR BALLOON PILOT

OVERVIEW

Flying across open fields, rolling hills, rivers and plains—silently drifting with the wind, free as a bird. Who *wouldn't* want to learn how to pilot one of these lighter-than-air devices—and get *paid* for it!

But there's a lot more to being a commercial hot-air balloon pilot than climbing into a basket and throwing the rope over the side. The Wizard of Oz might have made it look simple—but remember, he ended up in Oz by accident, and he didn't have the skill to leave.

To be a balloon pilot, you'll need lots of training. You'll start by attending ground school to learn important basics about flying a hot-air balloon. You'll learn about what you can and can't do as a balloon pilot. You'll learn how to read and use navigation charts, how to read weather reports, and how to recognize weather conditions that might affect your flight. You'll also learn about the operating procedures of hot-air balloons—how to handle the balloon on the ground, and how to inflate it. You'll practice preflight checks, how to take off and ascend, how to descend and land, what needs to be done after the flight, and what to do in an emergency situation.

Depending on where you live, you might be able to take classes to learn this information, or you could take a home study course. For your pilot's certificate, you'll need to take a 60-question written exam on the material, and you need a score of at least 70 percent to pass.

Of course, a lot of your training will take place in the air. To earn your commercial certificate, you need to have at least 35 hours of flight time as a pilot, and at least 20 of those hours must be in a balloon. The remaining time can be in other aircraft. You need to take two solo flights, two flights at least one hour long, and a flight to 3,000 feet above the takeoff point. After your in-air training, you'll have an oral exam and a test flight. During the test flight you will take an FAA examiner for a ride lasting at least one hour.

Michael Gianetti, hot-air balloon pilot

Michael Gianetti's entrance into the world of hot-air ballooning may sound strange to some people. But actually, it's the way that Gianetti and other balloon pilots recommend. "I got started chasing balloons," says Gianetti. When it landed, he talked to the pilot and ended up working as a crew member. He enjoyed ballooning so much that he decided to become a private pilot; that was 17 years ago. A year later he earned a commercial certificate and started flying for Life Cycle Balloon Adventures in Boulder, Colorado. Today, Gianetti is the owner of Life Cycle Balloons.

Gianetti left the safety and security of a good paying job in corporate America to do what he does, and he truly loves it. He enjoys that every flight is unique, and every flight is a challenge. "I get to see people having fun, people at their best," says Gianetti. And that's one of the things he likes best about his job.

Most balloon pilots—and even those with balloon companies—won't get rich at it, and they won't retire from it, Gianetti admits. Most pilots and even company owners have other jobs, some in ballooning and some in other fields. In addition to being a pilot, Gianetti is an instructor, a hot-air balloon dealer, and a certified inspector and repairman.

"Ballooning involves lots of early morning and hard work," he says. "Crew first, before you start spending money [on lessons and equipment]. Get a good feel for it, and make sure that you like it. And, get a ride if you can."

Any hot-air balloon pilot with a commercial rating can give flight lessons. There are also flight schools that offer the training you need to get your certificate. If you enroll in a full-time flight school, you can complete your training in as little as three to five weeks. If you work on your training part time, it will probably take you three to six months, depending on your progress and the weather. Your training will cost between $4,000 and $6,000.

Some instructors trade flight time and instruction for your work as a member of the ground crew. There are other benefits to working as a member of the crew— many companies want you to have extra flight time and experience before flying passengers. In fact, the more experience you have, the better—and working as a crew member is a great way to get that experience. As a crew member, you'll learn all the ins and outs of the balloon that will help make you a more successful pilot.

Once you have your commercial pilot certificate, you'll probably begin your career flying for someone else. Eventually, you'll probably want to buy your own equipment. Unfortunately, that's not cheap: A good, small, used balloon costs $10,000 to $20,000. A large balloon capable of carrying several passengers at a time can cost $20,000 to $40,000 or more. You'll also need to pay for a chase vehicle and a trailer, propane, insurance, crew salaries, and advertising.

Then, it's up, up, and away! As a hot-air balloon pilot, you'll join the ranks of more than 10,250 such pilots in the United States.

Pitfalls

Depending on the weather in your area, the economy, and many other factors, you might not make enough money working only as a hot-air balloon pilot to completely support yourself. And, while hot-air ballooning is relatively safe, there is always the possibility of a crash.

Perks

You'll never have to work in the rain. When you are at work, you will have a breathtaking, bird's-eye view of the area where you live or work. If you are an owner, you can pretty much set your own schedule by not scheduling flights on days you want off, or by hiring another pilot for flights on those days.

Get a Jump on the Job

Even though you cannot get a commercial certificate until you are 18 years old, you can get a student pilot's certificate at 14 years old and a private pilot's certificate at 16 years old. There are several other things you can do to get involved with and learn more about hot-air ballooning before you're able to take your first passengers for a ride.

Look for a hot-air balloon club in your area, and get as involved in the club as you can. If there aren't any clubs in your area, check with commercial hot-air balloon pilots and businesses offering balloon rides. You might be able to get a job, and a lot of experience, working on the ground crew.

Join the Balloon Federation of America's Junior Balloonist program, for kids between the ages of 7 and 18. Among the advantages of joining are scholarships, an annual balloon camp, along with other opportunities to get involved with the sport of ballooning.

HURRICANE HUNTER

OVERVIEW

As hurricane season approaches, people in coastal areas begin to prepare for the possibility that a bad storm may hit their area, stocking up on supplies, taping up windows, and making plans in case their area is evacuated. While citizens scurry around in preparation, the nation's "hurricane hunters" are also gearing up—but these men and women actually go out to face the storm. They are the 53rd Weather Reconnaissance Squadron (53rd WRS), and hurricane season—June 1 through November 30—is their busiest time of year.

Hurricane hunters are responsible for gathering information about tropical disturbances in the Atlantic, Caribbean, and Gulf of Mexico, tracking the center of the disturbance and measuring maximum winds. This information—which satellites can't provide—is then sent on to the National Hurricane Center in Miami.

The 53rd WRS is actually part of the 403rd Wing, located at Keesler Air Force Base in Biloxi, Mississippi. All hurricane hunters are members of the Air Force Reserves, and half of them also work full time as Air Reserve technicians (ARTs) available at all times to fly a mission.

There are 20 aircrews in the 53rd WRS. Each six-member crew is made up of two pilots, a flight engineer, a navigator, an aerial recon weather officer (ARWO) and a dropsonde operator. When called to duty, a team of hunters will take off in one of ten C-130 aircraft.

These workhorses aren't reinforced to deal with the conditions in which they fly, but they have been adapted for weather reconnaissance with computer equipment to collect weather data. The ARWO then takes data, checks its accuracy, and analyzes it to plot a course taking the airplane into the eye of the

Captain Chad Gibson, hurricane hunter

"You never know what to expect from a storm," says hurricane hunter Captain Chad Gibson, who has a degree in meteorology from Florida State University. "I've loved flying and aviation since I was a child. This is the perfect combination of science and flying. And it's unique, something else I've always enjoyed."

When flying a storm mission, Gibson and the other members of the team might fly for 10 to 12 hours at a time. Add to that the pre-flight and post-flight time, and he's looking at a 14- to 16-hour day. In addition to collecting and relaying weather information, the team is sometimes called on to help locate a boat lost in the storm. A second set of eyes from the sky is sometimes enough to spot the lost vessel, whose coordinates are then sent to the U.S. Coast Guard. Missions are exciting and adventurous, Gibson adds, but they're so busy that there isn't time to be afraid.

The amount of time in school and training is probably the biggest sacrifice someone would have to make to become a hurricane hunter. To monitor the weather as Gibson does, you'd need to have a degree in meteorology. "Learn as much math as you can," Gibson recommends. "It's the basis for a lot of things in science and physics. And read. Never stop learning."

Being a hurricane hunter takes persistence, determination, and tenacity. "You can do anything," Gibson said. "Don't sell yourself short, and don't take no for an answer."

storm. Once inside the eye of the storm, the dropsonde operator, who is a weather specialist, drops a sonde (a special instrument for collecting weather information). In addition to the six-man crew, each plane can carry up to 15 more people; missions might include a meteorologist, project scientist, cloud physicist, and radar specialist. Occasionally members of the media are able to accompany the hurricane hunters.

If you want to become a hurricane hunter, the first thing you need to do is to choose your specialty—pilot, navigator, ARWO, flight engineer, or dropsonde operator. You can start pursuing some of these jobs right after high school, but others require a college degree. This is why you really need to have an idea of what you want to do so you can make arrangements to meet the requirements.

If you are interested in working as a full-time hurricane hunter as an ART, you need to apply to the Air Force Reserve Command Special Examining Unit.

Once you've decided on a job, met the requirements, and been accepted into the Air Force Reserves, that's when the fun and the work begin! Your training will start with Basic Military (if you're enlisted personnel) or Officer Training School (for officer candidates). That means four months of training at Maxwell Air Force Base, near Montgomery, Alabama.

After basic training, you'll participate in a three-day class to learn how your body reacts to the stress of flying. You'll go through an altitude chamber to experience the pressure changes that happen at high altitudes. This is part of the formal training for pilots and navigators.

Depending on the job you're training for, you might be required to attend a formal school for more training. Depending on your specialty, this school may run a few months to more than one year, full time.

As an aircrew member, you'll also be required to attend survival school. That means three weeks of Basic Combat Survival at Fairchild Air Force Base in Spokane, Washington, where you'll put your skills to the test during a week in the Cascade Mountains. Finally, you'll spend four days in Florida learning water survival.

You'll still need to do some specialized in-house training, but you're officially a hurricane hunter now. If you're a traditional, part-time reservist, you'll probably have another full-time job. Your annual two-week training will be scheduled during the summer peak of hurricane season, but you might be called on to fly missions at other times as well.

Pitfalls

Although the 53rd WRS has flown more than 100,000 incident-free hours, there is always a risk associated with flying-related jobs. Most of the reservists live in the Gulf Coast area, so it may be necessary for you to relocate.

Perks

As a reservist, you'll receive a nice paycheck to supplement the income from your full-time job. You might be eligible for government money to help pay for college or additional training. You'll have the opportunity to see and experience things that most people can only dream about. Your work will help save the lives of people in the path of a hurricane.

Get a Jump on the Job

If you want to hunt hurricanes, stay in school, do your best, and graduate. Study for the Reservist's entrance exam (AFOQT or ASVAB). Check your local library or bookstore for books to help you prepare. Start a training program that includes strengthening and aerobic exercise to prepare you for Basic Military Training. If you're interested in a pilot/co-pilot position, consider getting your private pilot's certificate. Be well-rounded: Join in school activities, pursue hobbies, and take advantage of volunteer opportunities.

LAKE MAIL CARRIER

OVERVIEW

While being a postal worker may not sound like a particularly adventurous career, in some remote parts of the country the job can get mighty interesting. Lake mail carriers deliver mail to remote areas accessible by lake, and have a job that combines the pleasures of boating and daily interaction with the lake community.

You may be surprised to learn that not all mail is delivered by U.S. mail carriers working for the U.S. Postal Service. Some mail carriers in hard-to-reach or extremely isolated areas instead work for private companies that contract with the government to deliver the mail. Lake mail carriers are included in this group.

Lake mail carriers get up early to gather the mail and packages and stock the mail boat. Then they cast off on a trip around the lake and its islands. Depending on the size of the mail route or lake, it may be necessary to make more than one mail run per day to cover all the mail stops. On smaller stops, the carrier simply hands the mailbag to whoever arrives at the dock to pick it up; larger islands have mailboxes on the dock.

Hand-canceling letters on board is one of the primary duties of the mail carrier. The rest of the job description reads pretty much like any other mail clerk at a typical U.S. post office—arranging mail in the order of delivery, delivering letters, selling stamps, handling packages and express and priority mail. In addition, the floating mail car-

AT A GLANCE

Salary Range

About $9.25 an hour.

Education/Experience

College degree helpful; high school diploma required.

Personal Attributes

Courteous, tactful, with a good memory and the ability to read rapidly and accurately. Ability to handle a boat essential; also must be strong, able to lift and handle mail sacks weighing 70 pounds.

Requirements

U.S. citizenship or permanent resident status; 18 years of age; passage of a physical, drug test, and test that measures speed and accuracy at checking names and numbers; and ability to memorize procedures.

Outlook

Because of the large number of qualified applicants, stiff competition is expected and employment is expected to shrink due to declining mail volume and increasing automation.

riers gather mail from dock mailboxes to return to the post office.

Mail boats also sometimes carry paying passengers—the occasional daytrippers to or from the islands, or tourists who simply want to ride around the lake and enjoy the scenery.

At Lake Winnipesaukee, New Hampshire, the lake mail carrier delivers mail to some of the more than 274 islands in the 72-square-mile lake that aren't connected by bridge to mainland New Hampshire. The service was established by an act of Congress in 1916, and the *Sophie C.*—a 76-foot all-steer vessel—is the only floating post office in the United

Ed Touhey, lake mail carrier

People on the islands look forward to the arrival of the mail boat," says Ed Touhey, a retired school guidance counselor now working as mail carrier aboard the *Sophie C.* In the past, the mail boat carried newspapers, fruits, and vegetables, but now that most islands have electricity, telephone, and Internet service, the boat focuses on mail, passengers, and ice cream. Because there are no grocery stores on most of the unbridged islands, residents find it difficult to haul ice cream to their island by boat and get there without having a box of mush. For that reason, most of the island youngsters wait to buy their ice cream directly from the mail agent, when the mail boat arrives. Likewise, the island dogs have learned that the arrival of the mail boat means dog biscuits—and many gather to greet the carriers and get their treat.

"A lot of people really count on the mail boat," Touhey says. "It's a social call as much as a business call. They start gathering 15 minutes before you get there—parents, kids, dogs. We're always sure to have dog bones with us."

Touhey spent childhood summers on the lake at camp, and when he got married he and his wife bought land on the lake. After he retired, he'd see the boat go by, and people would wave. It seemed like an enjoyable way to earn a living.

"It's laid-back territory around here," Touhey says. "There's no stress. People are relaxed, they'll wave—down in the city, nobody waves." When he had the opportunity to retire, Touhey contacted the Lake Winnipesaukee Flagship Co. to see if there might be an opening on the *Sophie C.* As a sailor with his own boat, Touhey already knew the lake, which was a major point in his favor. "This lake is difficult to navigate if you don't know your way around," he says, "with lots of shoals. Boats go aground." He was hired at first to work the ticket booth, but the owners soon noticed Touhey's outgoing style, and realized he'd work well on the boat.

"I'm a real people person," Touhey says. "I really enjoy meeting people, answering questions about life on Lake Winnipesaukee."

States that has been assigned its own cancellation stamp. The *Sophie C.* can carry 125 passengers, plus a skipper, the mail agent, and a deckhand—plus all the mail and packages they can squeeze on board.

If you're interested in being a lake mail carrier, you'll need to contact the local company with the contract for handling the mail for the lake. Because it's not a government job, there's no civil service exam. But you do need to know quite a lot about navigating lakes, which are pock-marked with hidden underwater obstacles.

When a vacancy occurs, the company might start you off selling tickets for the boat ride. Eventually, when an opening comes up, you might be selected as mail carrier or boat skipper.

Relatively few people become mail carriers on these boats because of keen competition; it's not surprising that most entrants transfer from other occupations, or get hired in retirement.

Pitfalls

While delivering mail on the lake can be idyllic in beautiful summer weather, during a storm there can be heavy rain, with waves cresting at six or seven feet. The work is also seasonal; no mail is delivered once the lake ices up.

Perks

It can be an enormously satisfying life, if you love the water and enjoy chatting with people. Much more than most postal carriers, lake mail carriers interact almost constantly with the public. Once the mail is delivered, carriers can spend most of the day on their own, relatively free from direct supervision.

Get A Jump on the Job

Most mail-carrying boats on the lakes hire teens or college students for the summer to help on board. Consider applying for one of these jobs to see how you like the boating life.

LOBSTERMAN

OVERVIEW

It may seem like a romantic job, those individuals who make their living from the harvest of *Homarus americanus* in the waters of the northeastern seaboard of the United States. It's certainly a lot of hard work—and government regulation is making it harder and more frustrating for the commercial lobsterman.

If you're working as a lobsterman, you'll get up by 4 a.m. to start out early on your boat. When you reach your traps, the automatic hauler that brings up the traps from the bottom of the ocean is set in gear. A buoy is snared with a gaff hook and the line is passed over the snatch block and the hydraulic pot hauler. When the hauler is turned on, the line is pulled in by the pot hauler. The hauler is stopped when the trap is close enough to be brought aboard, and then restarted to retrieve the next trap.

This is the dangerous part—fingers have been lost by getting caught in the equipment. One lone lobsterman using an older hauler got his arm caught so badly he was forced to cut it off to free himself.

On large deep-water boats it's not uncommon to check 40 traps, with almost a mile between the buoys.

As you remove the lobsters from the traps, you'll measure potential keepers and band the legal catches (or *legals*). Regulations are tight in New England. Lobsters can't be too small or too big—you have to measure the carapace (body) of a lobster to check. Lobsters must be handled carefully (roughness can make the lobsters

drop a claw) as they are dropped into the "live tank"—a part of the boat designed to hold about 1,300 pounds. An average run these days may net 400 pounds of chicken lobsters (about 1 to 1.5 pounds each). "Shorts" (lobsters that are too small) and pregnant lobsters are tossed back over the side to be caught another day.

Then you bait the traps again, and the captain resets the trap line. This is another hard part—setting traps in the water without tangling with another lobsterman's line.

On the way back in, the boat gets a thorough scrub-down. Once you arrive at the buyer's dock, you open the hatches on the live tank and get ready to off-load the catch, scooping out the lobsters and

Phil Doucette, Maine lobsterman

Like his uncle and cousins before him, Phil Doucette of Kittery has been harvesting lobsters from the cold Maine waters for years. Sailing on his boat, *Chrissie D,* Doucette hauls 800 traps per trip—down from the 2,000 he used to have before the government started meddling in his business. Declaring the Maine waters overfished, the government stepped in and limited traps for commercial fisherman (while increasing the state's own ability to sell licenses to tourists). "It galls me to no end," Doucette says of Maine's actions.

His oldest son is going to college to be a pharmacist, but his middle and younger son intend to follow him into the lobster business. Because their father is already a commercial lobsterman, after they've served their two-year apprenticeship they can get a license without having to wait for the "5-to-1" rule. "In Maine, that means you go on a waiting list for a license, and you have to wait until five men ahead of you either die or give up their license before you can get one," he says. In the past, when Doucette's zone had only a "2-to-1" rule, it could take at least two years to wait for a license. With the 5-to-1 rule, it will take even longer.

Still, it's a business Doucette loves. Out on the water, "You'll see whales, you'll see seals," he says, "and you'll see sunrises like nobody else has ever seen."

carefully transferring them by hand to a tote.

Before heading back home, more bait is loaded for the next day.

Pitfalls

Lobstering can be dangerous. On a trawl, each trap is connected by a length of line, and as the boat moves forward, the weight of the previous traps drags the following traps into the water. If you get a hand or foot tangled in a line as it plays out, you could end up in the water with several hundred pounds of gear dragging you to the bottom. Fatalities can occur, especially to lobstermen out alone.

Perks

Being your own boss, the independence of running your own boat, and the pleasure of being out on the water are all some of the best parts of this job.

Get a Jump on the Job

Fascinated by lobstering? Learn more about lobsters and their conservation by applying for an internship at the New England Aquarium, which focuses on researching the biology, behavior, and physiology of lobsters. At the aquarium, larval and juvenile lobsters are studied to better understand their growth, nutrition, development, and disease. (Check it out at their Web site: http://www.neaq.org/community/intern/teen.index.html.)

LOGGER

OVERVIEW

Back in the 19th century, logging was a rough-and-ready trade fraught with danger and lots of hard work. With the lack of power tools, felling the giant virgin forests required brawn—and plenty of it. In fact, at the height of the logging era, it wasn't uncommon for lumberjacks to eat thousands of calories a day to give them the energy needed to do their job. And while today's lumberjacks (more commonly called loggers) don't need to eat quite the same carbohydrate-rich diet as their 1800s counterparts, logging is still very hard, physically demanding work. Even with the many mechanical inventions that have made some parts of the logging process easier and more efficient, chopping down trees still requires lots of manual labor.

Logging crews generally include four to eight people. *Fallers* cut the trees down. Because of the danger involved and the expertise and experience required, fallers are the highest paid members of a logging crew. After the tree is down, a *bucker* will remove the top and branches, and then cut (*buck*) the log into shorter pieces. A *choke setter* then attaches steel cables or chains (called *chokers*) around the logs so they can be moved to a landing area. There the logs are separated and loaded onto trucks. *Logging equipment operators* work in the landing area, moving the logs around and lifting and loading them onto the trucks. A crew might have one or two fellers, a bucker, one or two tractor operators to drag the trees to a

landing area, and an equipment operator to load the logs onto trucks.

There are a variety of other jobs in the logging industry. *Log sorters* and *markers* sort the logs by species and size, and then mark them to show who owns them. *Debarkers* run the machines that remove the bark from the logs. *Log graders* and *scalers* inspect the logs for defects, measure the volume, and determine the market value of the logs.

Some logging workers specialize in one area of the logging process, but with time on the job, most workers learn how to do each of the jobs.

If you have a yen to fell trees for a living, you'll start your career as a logger

Jim Gahlsdorf, logger

Unlike many logging company owners, Jim Gahlsdorf doesn't come from a logging family. "I chose a career in forestry when I was in junior high because I wanted to be outside," Gahlsdorf explains. Eventually, he got a summer job working as a choke setter and liked it. After earning a degree in forestry, Gahlsdorf worked with a consulting company for 11 years before deciding to return to the forest. Today, he runs a logging company that employs 50 to 60 workers. But even with the responsibilities that come with running a company, Gahlsdorf still gets out into the forest as often as possible. He spends about half his time in the office figuring jobs and dealing with the business end of his operation, and the other half out in the forest.

"I like the challenge of it," he says, "but it's changed across the spectrum since I began. The challenge has changed from cutting down trees to people management."

Gahlsdorf warns that the competition is tough and it can be tough to find enough money to start a logging business. "Spend some time learning on someone else's nickel," he advises, recommending that potential loggers join a state logging association for the networking opportunities and support systems they provide. Any experience at all—knowing how to operate a chain saw, experience working outdoors, an agriculture background—really helps, along with any experience that will help prepare you for the long days working in all sorts of conditions that you'll face as a logger. "Experience doing outdoor physical work is a definite positive," he adds, as is a good work ethic. Good hand-eye coordination is also important for anyone handling logging tools. "Some of the equipment is pretty sophisticated," he notes, "and you need some troubleshooting skills to operate it."

Someone who is passionate about working in the forest environment, moving logs, and doing physical work would find logging an ideal job. "It's a lot of work, and it's not for everyone," he says. "To be successful, you have to like what you're doing."

doing manual labor with a logging crew. You'll be responsible for carrying the tools and equipment, clearing brush, and loading and unloading logs. You'll learn the skills needed to advance to other positions from more experienced loggers on your crew. You'll learn how to operate the logging equipment and how to work safely in what can be a very dangerous environment.

As a logger, you'll face many dangers on the job. The large machinery that makes your job easier also can cause serious injury if not used correctly, or if something goes wrong. The noise from the equipment can eventually damage your hearing, so it's important to take precautions. Strong winds make it very dangerous to fell trees,

and sometimes windy conditions get so bad, they'll stop your crew from working. Muddy conditions, roots, and vines create problems not only for you, but for the logging equipment too. If that isn't enough, you'll also have to deal with poisonous plants, bugs, and snakes—plus brush and brambles, heat, and humidity.

While there aren't usually any education requirements to be a logger, training programs are becoming more common. Programs vary from state to state, but they usually cover topics such as safety procedures, management skills, endangered species, and reforestation. If you participate in a training program, it may lead to logger certification.

Skilled, experienced loggers eventually may become crew leaders, or they may move into a management position with a logging company. Other loggers decide to open their own logging company; 20 to 25 percent of loggers are self-employed.

Pitfalls

In addition to the many on-the-job dangers that loggers face, some logging operations are seasonal. Even though almost every state has some type of logging operations, it may be necessary for you to relocate to find a job. About 37 percent of all loggers work in the southeastern part of the United States, and another 30 percent work in the northwest.

Perks

For people who enjoy the great outdoors, a career as a logger offers the opportunity to spend a lot of time outdoors, often in beautiful, rugged terrain.

Get a Jump on the Job

Take advantage of any vocational opportunities your school offers in forestry-related areas, such as general forestry, conservation, or harvesting. Check with logging operations in your area for summer jobs. If you think you might want to run your own logging company some day, take some business classes in high school or college.

MERCHANT MARINER

OVERVIEW

Shipping has played a fundamental part in America's history. Ships brought the early explorers and settlers to this country's shores, and then ferried much-needed supplies to those settlers—supplies that helped early Americans survive the harsh winters and build the first towns. For many years, shipping was the *only* way to get goods and resources to and from other countries.

Even today, shipping plays a major role in the economy. Enter the U.S. Merchant Marines (USMM), a fleet of privately-owned ships that transports people, products, and natural resources across the United States and around the world. The men and women who serve on board these vessels work on ships traveling on the high seas, the Great Lakes, and along coastal and inland waters, performing a wide range of jobs.

Ordinary seamen stand watch while the ship is in port or at sea. They're responsible for general deck maintenance like cleaning, painting, and preservation. *Able-bodied seamen* perform the same tasks as ordinary seamen, but they're also responsible for things such as operating underway replenishment rigs, cargo handling, and helicopter flight-deck operations. *Utilitymen (food handlers)* clean and maintain the staterooms and passageways, help with the food handling, and assist the chief steward. *Wipers* are responsible for general engine department maintenance,

ship maintenance (cleaning, painting, and preservation), and assisting with machinery repairs.

Captain Mike Surgalski, merchant mariner

At how many jobs can you go to sleep at night and wake up someplace different every day?" asks Merchant Marine Captain Mike Surgalski.

A 1979 graduate of the U.S. Merchant Marine Academy, he has spent much of his career on and around the Great Lakes, spending two years working on Great Lakes tankers, and 11 years working on passenger boats in the Detroit River, near Lake Erie. Today, Surgalski is an instructor in the Deck Officer Program at the Great Lakes Maritime Academy at Northwestern Michigan College in Traverse City.

Becoming a merchant mariner was an almost natural choice for Surgalski. "As a kid, I watched the ships on the St. Clair River. When I got to high school, I decided I wanted to work on those ships." And once Surgalski was on board, he liked that things were constantly changing. "There is no such thing as an average day for merchant mariners."

Surgalski also enjoyed the camaraderie among the crew. And while it can be tough to be gone for long periods of time, "It's a very good way to make a living." To students, Surgalski advises, "Be patient and stick with it. It's worth it in the end."

Fortunately, modern working conditions on board these ships have improved greatly from the early days of shipping. Most of the vessels today are air-conditioned. Soundproofing quiets the noisy machinery on board, and comfortable living quarters make working on these ships fairly pleasant. Crew members are able to keep in touch with family and friends back home via e-mail and telephones on the ship.

Crew members are not members of the U.S. military, but merchant marine officers have the option of becoming commissioned officers in the U.S. Naval Reserve, the Merchant Marine Reserve, or the Coast Guard Reserve. There are many benefits for those who decide to join the military, including financial incentives and training.

On the other hand, as members of the U.S. military, those commissioned officers may be called to active duty if needed—and they are obligated to complete their service to the U.S. military as a reservist. In addition, merchant marine vessels might be called on to transport troops or military goods during a war or other national emergency.

Still interested? There are lots of ways to get started in a career with the U.S. Merchant Marine. If you're interested in a deck or engineering officer position, one of the best ways to reach that goal is to attend the U.S. Merchant Marine Academy at Kings Point, New York. Like the other U.S. military academies, tuition at the Merchant Marine Academy is free. Candidates are appointed to the academy on a competitive basis, based on an allotted number of openings per state.

There are also six state maritime academies—but you'll have to pay tuition at these schools.

Upon completion of the four-year program offered by the academies, you'll receive a B.S. degree and a Coast Guard-issued license as a third mate (deck officer) or a third assistant engineer (engineering officer). You can become a deck or engineering officer without attending the academy, but it can take five to eight years to get the required experience, and even then it's hard to pass the written exam without some formal schooling.

Although there are many jobs on the ships that don't require any formal education or experience, attending one of the union-operated schools might help you get your first job at sea, and it might help you advance in your career. You'll start out as an ordinary seaman, and you'll be assigned to the deck, engine room, or as a steward. Before applying for any job, you'll need to get your merchant mariner documents.

Many of the jobs on merchant marine vessels are union jobs, and are filled through the union hiring halls. Therefore it may be necessary for you to join one (or more) of the maritime labor unions.

Pitfalls

Merchant mariners sometimes have long periods of unemployment between jobs, and some jobs are seasonal. Although it rarely happens, there's always the possibility that an accident will force you to abandon ship in the middle of the ocean. By necessity, merchant mariners don't see their families and friends for long periods of time, and while at sea they may have to contend with bad storms and inclement weather.

Perks

In addition to excellent pay, most jobs provide 13 days (or more) of paid vacation for each 30 days worked. For some jobs, you'll get a day of vacation for each day aboard ship. Merchant mariners have the opportunity to travel the inland waterways, the Great Lakes, or around the world on the high seas.

Get a Jump on the Job

There are several high schools and maritime-related organizations where you can get a head start on your career. For more information, check out http://www.marad.dot.gov/acareerafloat/highschools.htm. Some of the positions have individual requirements, qualifications, or certifications. For example, merchant mariner radio officers must pass the Federal Communications Commission (FCC) license exam. You might want to investigate various positions that you are interested in for specific requirements.

MOUNTAIN GUIDE

OVERVIEW

Imagine taking a group of people into the wilderness of the High Sierra, creating lasting memories where the food was fantastic, the guide became a friend, and the scenery refreshed the soul.

Many mountain guides live their lives this way, planning the highest quality adventure travel trips for their clients. They're working in a job they love based on shared dreams, fulfilling work, community, and a lifestyle where the passion for wilderness adventure has become their career.

Most mountain guides love the mountains they know so well, and they find great joy in sharing the mountains with others. The job begins at the planning stage, where a mountain guide arranges for camping and climbing equipment, transportation to the site, and for any necessary medical or other personnel. Before choosing an ascent site, guides must understand how well the clients climb and where they've climbed before.

Countries in the European Alps require completion of a vigorous training and examination program before leading a client on a rope. But in the United States, training of professional mountain guides has been loosely organized and inconsistently regulated. While some guide services conduct in-house training, few guides have had any formal, comprehensive training. As a result, anyone can claim to be a competent guide.

The American Mountain Guides Association (AMGA) is the only U.S.

organization to promote a uniform, comprehensive, nationwide training program for mountain guides at the international level. Choosing a guide certified by the AMGA ensures that the guide has demonstrated the minimum acceptable level of specific skills that separate the professional guide from the recreational climber. Each certified guide has met an internationally recognized standard of expertise and professionalism and actively participates in continuing

Jim Williams, mountain guide

Jim Williams has been climbing, guiding, and studying the world's major peaks for almost 30 years. The owner and founder of Exploradus since 1985 (formerly Professional Mountain Guides), Williams has reached the summit of six of the world's seven highest mountains and covered almost every country in Asia, South America, Europe, Africa, and Antarctica.

"I began my career by exploring mountains at age 14," he explains, "and I continued my interest in climbing and mountaineering while earning a geology degree from Rocky Mountain College in Montana." Today he lives in Jackson Hole, Wyoming, where he is a senior guide with Exum Mountain Guides during the summer.

As co-leader of the successful 1982 Rudshe Konka Expedition in central China, Williams made the first ascent of one of China's most difficult ice climbs. In 1989, Jim led the International Overland Expedition, the historic cross-country ski expedition to the South Pole. He also led the first American crossing of the Patagonia Ice Cap in 1991. In 1993, 1997, and 1999 Williams guided a successful winter ascent of Ama Dablam in Nepal, and in 2004 led the Everest Extreme—a NASA/Yale medical research expedition.

"I'm an accomplished mountaineer," William says, "but my natural curiosity has inspired me to absorb the beauty and culture of the many countries I've explored."

education throughout his or her career. In addition, an AMGA-certified guide meets or exceeds high standards in areas such as client care, risk management, first aid, avalanche awareness, and high-angle rescue training.

Someone who is a fully certified International Federation of Mountain Guide Associations (IFMGA) mountain guide has permission to guide in nearly any IFMGA-member country, including Peru, New Zealand, Canada, and most European nations.

The U.S. Mountain Guides Association offers an endorsement program for guides in the rock, alpine, and ski guiding disciplines who have passed an AMGA exam. A *mountain guide* is the highest level of United States Mountain Guides Association (USMGA) endorsement and the only certification recognized internationally. An endorsed mountain guide has passed the highest-level exams in all the guiding disciplines. An *alpine*

guide has been examined in all the skill areas required to work in the alpine environment, including climbing in glaciers, ice, or complex mountainous terrain. A *ski mountaineering guide* is endorsed for ski guiding on all ski terrain including glaciers.

The USMGA endorsement program ensures that guides have been highly trained and can meet the established standard in areas such as climbing ability, technical guiding skills, safety management, rescue, and first aid. The USMGA endorsement is only good for the discipline in which the guide has been examined.

There are a number of courses and exams you can take in order to get your USMGA certifications in the United States; the American Mountain Guide Association is responsible for running these programs in the United States. It's possible with enough climbing and guiding experience to sometimes skip over a course or one of the first-level exams. Also, endorsed guides who were certified in another country may have followed a different course structure. This education process generally takes years of training and hard work to complete and the end result is a better guide. The exams serve as a form of quality control, ensuring that the guide has been well trained, meets the standard, and is ready to guide the public.

Pitfalls

While it may seem glamorous, there are very real dangers in this occupation, which also involves lots of hard work. If you and a client are 600 feet off the ground, 500 feet from the top of a mountain, and a violent summer storm rolls in, getting out of this potentially dangerous situation calls upon your expertise and training. Climbing skills alone aren't enough; guiding experience and training, as well as evaluation of guiding-specific skills, are essential to reduce potential hazards. Guides spend their working hours outdoors in all kinds of weather. Their working hours are usually long, and they may have to carry heavy backpacks, cook their own meals over open campfires, and sleep on the ground.

Perks

For folks who love to climb mountains, what could be better than leading expeditions for others all over the world? The independence and challenge, plus the opportunity to meet others with similar interests, make this career opportunity for the right person.

Get a Jump on the Job

If you're interested in climbing mountains and hope someday to become a mountain guide, there are all sorts of opportunities you can explore right now that will come in handy later on. First of all, get out there and start climbing! You can start small, but any experience is helpful.

Then consider an internship at a mountain guide school. For example, the Acadia Mountain Guides Climbing School in Maine offers 5- to 12-week internship/apprenticeships for qualified college and high school students interested in the fields of adventure education, mountain guiding, guide service management, and outdoor retail business management. Typical internships involve exposure to the various aspects of operating an outdoor program and adventure leadership center. In addition to their daily activities, interns are expected to develop a focused project. (For information, see the Web site at http://www.acadiamountainguides.com/home/jobs.html.)

There are literally hundreds of outdoor adventure schools and mountain-climbing trips designed expressly for teens. Check out a sample on the Internet. Sign up for as many courses as you can (not just in mountain climbing, but also in wilderness adventure, wilderness medicine, rock climbing, alpine rescue, and so forth). The more experience you have, the better you'll be prepared for a career as a mountain guide!

NAVY SEAL

OVERVIEW

If you love the sea and yearn to protect your country, the SEALs—an elite group of men who conduct the U.S. Navy's special operations missions—might be for you. Making up less than 1 percent of all navy personnel, the SEALs can successfully perform covert missions that larger units might not be able to do without being detected.

SEAL missions include combatting terrorism, running special reconnaissance, collecting warfare information, providing security assistance, running counter-drug operations, and recovering naval personnel. Navy SEALs are unique from other military special forces—they are the only special operations teams that strike from and then return to the sea.

Each SEAL team is assigned an area of operation in the desert, arctic, woodland, or jungle. Team members then receive special training to deal with and work in that specific terrain. Desert teams learn how to work in extreme heat, while arctic teams learn winter warfare techniques. Woodland and jungle teams learn camouflage techniques to help them blend into their surroundings. Working in and on the sea, in the air, and on the land, SEALs are trained to adjust to and work in any environment. In fact, that's where the name SEAL comes from: SEa, Air, Land.

To become a Navy SEAL, you'll start by passing the Armed Services Vocational Aptitude Battery (ASVAB) with the required scores. You'll select the position you want to eventually train for (called a source rate), you'll sign your SEAL Challenge Contract, and enlist in the U.S. Navy.

AT A GLANCE

Salary Range
Varies depending on rank and length of service, with extra pay for special skills and assignments (up to $340/month dive pay, up to $225/month jump pay, up to $150/month demolition pay, and up to $225/month special duty assignment pay). You can check out the current pay scale at http://www.dod.mil/dfas/money/milpay.

Education/Experience
High school diploma or high school equivalency is required. Check with a navy recruiter for more information.

Personal Attributes
Work well as a member of a team. Be able to adapt to any situation. Remain calm and level-headed in any situation. Must be in excellent physical condition.

Requirements
U.S. citizen. Twenty-eight years old or less (at 17, you'll need parental consent). Speak, read, and write English fluently. No more than two dependents. Single parents may not enlist in the Navy. Pass the Armed Services Vocational Aptitude Battery (ASVAB) test with a minimum combined score of 104 on the Arithmetic Reasoning (AR) and Verbal Expression (VE) sections, and a score of 50 or higher in the Mechanical Comprehension (MC) section. Pass a military entrance medical exam, physical fitness test, and a diving physical exam. Eyesight no worse than 20/40 in one eye and 20/70 in the other, must be correctable to 20/20. Normal color vision. The SEAL program is not open to women. Check with a navy recruiter for other requirements that may apply.

Outlook
Special operations teams play an important part in many military operations, including America's war on terror. As a result, there may be continued opportunities for qualified individuals interested in a career as a Navy SEAL.

Like all members of the military you'll go through basic or recruit training, also know as boot camp. Naval recruit training is held at the Great Lakes Naval Station near Chicago, Illinois. You'll start with several days of processing (called P-days), when you'll receive your clothing and training gear. You'll learn how to fold and store your items, how to make your bunk, and you'll get your navy haircut. You'll learn all the dos and don'ts of the navy—in short, you'll get ready for boot camp.

After P-week, you'll go through eight weeks of training to become a sailor. You'll work on physical conditioning and swimming and go through weapons training. In addition to your classroom training, you'll also get some real-world training on board the *Marlinspike*, an indoor land-bound trainer ship. The training is physically and mentally demanding, but for SEAL candidates, it's just a warm-up for the training to come.

After boot camp, you'll receive some basic training for the job position you selected. Then you'll go to Coronado, California, for six months of Basic Underwater Demolition/SEAL (known as BUD/S) training. BUD/S training starts with a five-week indoctrination period, where you'll get an introduction to SEAL training and techniques.

The First Phase (Basic Conditioning) lasts for eight weeks. During that time, you'll work on the physical conditioning required of a Navy SEAL. The third week of First Phase is known as "hell week." During that week you'll be pushed to your physical and mental limits with five and a half days of continuous training. During that training you'll get a maximum of four hours sleep total.

After First Phase you'll spend eight weeks in Second Phase, learning diving techniques. It's these weeks that separate you from other special operations forces. SEALs are the only special ops forces that go through dive training.

Third Phase is nine weeks of training in land warfare. You'll learn land navigation, small-unit tactics, marksmanship, explosives, and patrolling techniques. The last three and a half weeks are spent on San Clement Island where you'll put all your training to the test.

After some additional training, depending on your rating, you'll be assigned to a SEAL unit for six to 12 months of on-the-job training. After you receive your SEAL classification, you can complete additional training such as sniper school, dive supervision, tactical communications, and more.

Pitfalls

Depending on your specialty or your assignment, you might need to move away from family and friends. As with all military positions, there is a higher-than-average chance of being injured or killed in the line of duty.

Perks

Navy SEALs enjoy lots of benefits, including steady income, medical and dental insurance, two-and-a-half days of paid vacation a month (30 days a year), and a monthly allowance for uniforms, food, and housing. The government will also help pay for additional college or vocational technical training.

Get a Jump on the Job

Study for the ASVAB. Check your local library or bookstore for books to help your prepare for the test. Prepare for the physical requirements of the physical screen test, boot camp, and SEAL training. To help you train, the navy provides information

Mark "Cy" Divine, former Navy SEAL

When you're an old man with grandchildren, do you want them to say to you: 'Grandpappy, tell us about that last audit you did' or 'Grandpappy, tell us about your last mission in North Korea' ?" That was the question someone asked Mark "Cy" Divine back when he was 25, armed with an MBA and dissatisfied with his job as a certified public accountant. "I felt there had to be something else out there to develop me as a leader," Divine recalls. The Navy SEAL program seemed to be the answer to what he was looking for.

After completing Officer Candidate School, Divine entered SEAL training class no. 170. Of the 120 other men in his class, only 19 eventually graduated, with Divine as the Honor Man—number one in his class. Those numbers are pretty typical of a SEAL training class: About 80 percent of those who start training never make it through. For each class, about 2,000 men show some interest in becoming a SEAL. Some of those individuals are weeded out because they don't meet the requirements, and others are eliminated during the selection process. One of the mottos of the Navy SEALs is "Failure is not an option."

To become a SEAL, Divine says you need to have a creative warrior spirit. "You need the willpower to keep going when the going gets so brutal that people around you are dropping like flies," Divine explains. Candidates must be good swimmers, love the water, and be able to deal with the cold, because they'll be wet and cold for a good part of the six months of SEAL training. Martial arts, boxing, and wrestling teach useful skills for prospective candidates. "Navy SEALs are the ultimate cross-trainers!" Divine explains.

After serving eight years of active duty, Divine is now a reservist mobilized to active duty. "The esprit de corps was incredible," Divine remembers. "I was closer to my team members than I was to some of my family." In addition to the relationships, Divine was also fond of the travel he enjoyed as a SEAL. During his tenure, Divine visited more than 35 countries as part of his duties, and was on active duty about 10 months a year.

All that travel does carry a price. "It's exhausting, mentally and physically," he says, "And it's hard on relationships." Divine left active duty service when he got married in 1996. Today, he's founder and president of a SEALs Web site, http://www.NavySEALs.com.

For anyone considering becoming a Navy SEAL, Divine recommends that you first prepare yourself mentally and physically so when you make the call to the recruiter, you know exactly what you're getting into.

"It's an exciting and honorable career," Divine says. "It's risky and dangerous, but the rewards are significant. The character you gain and the type of person you become defines you for life. If you can succeed as a SEAL, you can do anything you want in life."

about the physical fitness standards, student preparation, nutrition, and more at http://www.navyseals.com/community/navyseals/navysealworkout_main.cfm.

The navy also offers a program for youths interested in becoming a Navy SEAL, or joining the navy in some other position. The Naval Sea Cadet Corps (NSCC) is for students ages 11 to 17. Students who participate in the program will get an introduction to Navy SEAL life. The program also helps students to build pride, patriotism, courage, athleticism, and self-reliance in a drug-free environment. Individuals who participate in the sea cadet program have no military obligation.

OUTWARD BOUND LEADER

OVERVIEW

Rappelling down a mountain, climbing a rope ladder, crossing a fast-moving river—outdoor education courses are popular ways for students to face their fears and triumph over challenges while relying on their fellow students. The premier outdoor education program is Outward Bound, first conceived in Great Britain in 1941. It has since become the premier adventure-based education program in the world.

During World War II, renowned educator Kurt Hahn developed programs to instill greater self-reliance and spiritual tenacity in young British seamen being torpedoed by German U-boats. He developed his progressive ideas first as founder of the Salem School in Germany, and later at Gordonstoun, a boarding school in Scotland, that soon became one of Britain's most distinguished and innovative schools. Hahn believed education must encompass both the intellect and character of a person, so in creating the first Outward Bound School, he expanded the concept of experiential learning to include real and powerful experience to gain self-esteem, the discovery of innate abilities, and a sense of responsibility toward others.

In the early 1950s, Josh Miner, an American who taught under Hahn at the Gordonstoun School, was inspired by Hahn's philosophy and founded the Outward Bound movement in the United States based on the principles of hands-on learning through outdoor adventure.

From the establishment of the Colorado Outward Bound School in 1961, outdoor education programs blossomed in the United States. With its nationwide system of wilderness schools and urban centers, Outward Bound USA helps people build confidence through personal achievement. New teachers typically must work for at least a season in the field to advance to be a full instructor.

As a teacher in a modern Outward Bound program, you would continue to use the wilderness as a classroom for self-discovery in one of four wilderness schools (Outward Bound West, Hurricane Island, Voyageur, and North Carolina), two independent urban centers (New York City Outward Bound Center and Thompson Island Outward Bound Education Center), or the primary and secondary school-

Billy Roos, former Outward Bound instructor

This Colorado carpenter was attracted to the life of an Outward Bound instructor where he could use his mountaineering skills to work with students. "I brought most of my experience with me to the program, although I got some more advanced aid training here," Roos recalls. "I was already experienced in the kind of courses I was doing—winter mountaineering courses." Roos loves being outside all the time, having the opportunity to interact with students and staff.

"The primary focus of Outward Bound is to encourage personal development and enhance skills in group interaction...You could do that under a table, but I taught these concepts in the mountains of Colorado."

Over the years, Roos says he received a significant amount of training. "Not all at once, not just one lesson, but over the entire time I worked, the skills you learn are constantly being upgraded."

Still, it's not necessarily an easy job. Almost all field instructors are seasonal, which can present a problem with employees trying to raise a family. "It was sometimes difficult when working seasonally, because you had to figure out what you were going to do when you were not working for Outward Bound," Roos recalled. "For me, it was always easy to work in the trades [as a carpenter], or for other outdoor organizations."

"It's not a great job unless you have the luxury of being able to work seasonally. Otherwise, it's low wages and poor working conditions, living out of a bag most of time, only working seasonally. It's not a lot different than some other migratory or seasonal jobs. On the other hand, it can provide some excellent experience in managing groups and in assuming a high degree of responsibility."

reform program, Expeditionary Learning Outward Bound.

Students come into the program from all over the country. The Outward Bound screening process tries to make sure that applicants understand what they are getting into, and that they are willing and able participants. Most actually are very anxious to participate, although occasionally students have been sent to the program by their parents without a clear idea of what they would be getting into.

As an instructor, your job is to encourage participants to build individual self-esteem and self-reliance through responsible risk-taking and hands-on involvement. You teach compassion through active participation within a team structure or through service projects. You also try to instill in students a sense of integrity that results in choices and actions that have a positive effect on society and the environment. You'll also help participants focus on self-knowledge, craftsmanship, tenacity, physical fitness, and teamwork. Leadership, acceptance of responsibility, and self-reliance are also important. Experiences are intentionally designed, presented, and reflected upon to instill values and promote skill mastery.

Pitfalls

The work is poorly paid and seasonal—lasting only three months out of the year—so it's difficult to make a living as an Outward Bound instructor. Living conditions are quite often fairly primitive.

Perks

If you love the outdoors and working with people (especially students), this can be an ideal career. Because they have the summers off, teachers in particular may find this a great way to spend a summer.

Get a Jump on the Job

Although Outward Bound typically hires only adults over age 21 because of car insurance issues, there are occasionally some intern jobs available. Otherwise, get lots of experience outdoors, in canoeing, mountain climbing, rock climbing, boating, swimming, or trail building.

PRIVATE INVESTIGATOR

OVERVIEW

Small, dark, cramped offices, stakeouts, trench coats, and hiding in the shadows to get the dirt on a suspect—the life of a private eye. Or at least that's what Hollywood might have you think. Real-world private investigator work might not be quite so glamorous, but it does have the potential to be an interesting career for the right individual.

As a private investigator or detective, you will find that each new job brings new tasks and challenges in collecting the information or evidence to meet the needs of your client. Many times investigators or detectives are hired by individuals, businesses, or lawyers to gather information. Thanks to computer databases and the Internet, sometimes the information you need can be found quickly. At other times, you'll need to resort to old-fashioned surveillance, and that can mean hours spent sitting in a car with a pair of binoculars, a camera, and a burger and fries—just waiting. Back at your desk, you might need to make phone calls or interview people to double-check the information you have collected.

After you've collected the evidence, you'll present it to your client. Depending on the circumstances, you might even be called to testify in court about the information and how you collected it.

Private investigators and detectives do all sorts of jobs for people. They're hired by employers to check the back-

ground history of a prospective employee. Lawyers use the services of detectives and investigators quite a bit. They might hire you to gather information to be used in personal injury cases, insurance claims and fraud, child custody battles, or workers' compensation claims. Divorce lawyers and individuals also hire private eyes, usually to prove or disprove infidelity. Other individuals hire private eyes to locate missing persons.

Marvin Powers, private investigator

I t's not all the drama of Tom Selleck [*Magnum, P.I.*], but there are some very rewarding moments," says private investigator Marvin Powers, who doesn't believe that television offers a true representation of what private investigators do. "P.I.s provide a special service that you can't get anywhere else."

"One of the best things a young person can do is to get on with a reputable company to build up your experience and credibility." Another excellent way to gain that experience is by working in law enforcement first. "You have a better chance at being successful if you've worked in law enforcement. People want to hire someone with credentials. But, the real test is in court, when you testify. You need credentials and experience or the attorney will eat you alive."

Powers, the owner of Florida Metro Investigations, earned his credibility and experience in his 26 years with the Daytona Beach Police Department, where he served as the chief of detectives. Among the things Powers likes about his job is that he's serving the public, just like in law enforcement, using the same skills.

To aspiring private investigators, Powers advises people to be honest in every single thing they do. "Don't ever compromise the truth," he warns, "because once you do, you're done. Be thorough; use your investigative sense and your common sense to put things together and make a conclusion based on the facts. The key to being a good PI is to use your deductive and inductive reasoning skills. But, above all, never compromise your honesty."

In most states, you'll need a license to work as a private investigator or detective, but the requirements to get a license vary greatly from state to state. Alabama, Alaska, Colorado, Idaho, Mississippi, and South Dakota have no statewide licensing requirements. Other states have very strict requirements to become licensed.

In some states, there is a minimum age requirement. For example, in Michigan you must be at least 25 years old to be eligible for a private investigator license. Some states require a certain number of hours of on the job experience, and many have an education requirement.

Even if your state doesn't have an educational requirement for licensing, you might find it helpful to take some classes in criminal justice, forensic science, and law enforcement. You might also be required to pass a written exam.

Private investigators and detectives aren't police officers, and generally they don't need to carry a gun. If you'll be working in a situation, such as a bodyguard, where you need to carry a weapon, there will be additional requirements for that permit.

Many law enforcement officers, military personnel, and federal agents move into a second career as a private investigator or detective. Because of their training, experience, and skills acquired on the job, they often meet all the requirements for licensing.

Pitfalls

There is stiff competition for jobs with very little turnover. Many entry-level jobs are part time. Private investigators often have to work irregular hours, including early mornings, late nights, weekends, and holidays, to collect the evidence they need.

Perks

About 40 percent of private investigators and detectives are self-employed. And even though being self-employed is hard work, it also lets you have a little more flexibility and freedom.

Get a Jump on the Job

After graduating from high school, consider getting some on-the-job experience working as a store detective while working on the requirements for a private investigator license in your state.

PYROTECHNICIAN

OVERVIEW

Those gorgeous half-hour fireworks shows on the Fourth of July never seem to last long enough for the audience, but that brief burst of sound and light magic is actually the result of hours of work to set up by trained pyrotechnicians—experts in creating special effects using fire and smoke.

Most fireworks pyrotechnicians spend long hours planning and building firework displays, a few minutes setting them off, and then more hours cleaning up afterwards. The job also may entail selling fireworks at stands, tents, and stores.

Most pyrotechnicians work for companies who produce fireworks displays for Fourth of July celebrations. On a typical day, a pyrotechnician might begin by arranging racks of firework mortars (the tubes usually made of high-density plastic) from which fireworks shells are shot. Once arranged, the pyrotechnician fills the mortars with shells and fuses, covering the shells with a tarp or aluminum foil to protect the shells and fuses from moisture and possible flying sparks. Next, the pyrotechnician hooks certain fuses hooked together so they go off at once. Once the preparation work is finished and it's time for the show, the pyrotechnician ignites the extremely fast-burning fuse with a flare or with an electronic firing system.

While it may seem like a glamorous job, it's important to remember that a small percentage of the time is spent actually firing off the effects. The rest of the time,

AT A GLANCE

Salary Range
About $150 day (for a 10- to 12-hour day) for apprentice pyrotechnicians; licensed pyrotechnicians earn a bit more. Pros for stunts and special effects firework displays can earn $30 to $65 an hour.

Education/Experience
Companies occasionally offer seminars and classes, but typically the job requires years of apprenticeship training on seasonal fireworks shows or interning with the few companies that do pyrotechnical film and stunt show special effects. Physics, chemistry, art, and music classes can help.

Personal Attributes
Must be safety-conscious, creative, willing to work hard, detail-oriented, careful, enthusiastic, and have a strong drive to learn.

Requirements
A state license is usually required for most work with fireworks; rules vary from state to state. For special effects, California (where most stunt and special effects pyrotechnicians work) requires pyrotechnicians to have at least two years of experience, letters of reference from licensed pyrotechnicians, and a passing grade on explosives and fireworks safety exam. Pyrotechnicians must be at least 21, have a clean criminal record, and no history of mental illness to obtain a license. Many cities also require a bond of a few hundred dollars to cover the fire department or ambulance. Pyrotechnicians need a variety of licenses in order to use explosives with certain kinds of detonators and to buy, sell, and transport fireworks and explosive materials.

Outlook
Fair. Although more people are hiring pyrotechnicians for weddings, family reunions, and birthday parties, the number of people who can afford professional fireworks displays is still small. Most fireworks displays are limited to Fourth of July celebrations; job openings for pyrotechnicians who specialize in special effects with fire or explosives are rare.

you're talking to clients, moving heavy objects, ordering parts, and designing and planning fireworks shows or special effects.

Enthusiasm, patience, determination, and a strong drive to learn are especially important in this profession, where entry-level work is often temporary and repetitive—but necessary. Because there aren't any training or degree programs strictly focusing on pyrotechnics, beginners must apprentice or intern before getting licensed to shoot off fireworks on their own. For example, New Hampshire pyrotechnicians must apprentice with a licensed shooter on 10 shoots (five with one licensed pyrotechnician, five with another) before becoming eligible for licensure. License requirements vary by state, type of fireworks, and how the effects will be used, but almost all require this initial apprenticeship period. Many states, such as New Hampshire, also require extra safety classes and training each year to maintain licensure.

A few pyrotechnicians focus on special effects, working with production companies to create safe and convincing effects in movies, TV, theme parks, stunt shows, theatre, concerts, and sporting events. These experts make much more money, and spend their time planning and orchestrating fires and explosions. Those who do this kind of work may spend their time setting up, igniting, and controlling small fires and explosions that on film look dramatic and larger than life, or working at a car stunt show, creating and controlling a wall of fire for a daredevil driver to race through during a live performance. Special effects fireworks experts set up and ignite large explosions or controlled fires, and setting up special effects by cutting away at film props

(such as miniature buildings) and placing explosives in the holes. Special effects pyrotechnicians also must test explosions to make sure they produce the correct effect on film.

Pyrotechnicians who work mainly with fireworks usually begin as volunteers, helping full-fledged pyrotechnicians mount fireworks displays on holidays. After acquiring enough experience to win the approval of local authorities, pyrotechnicians can land part-time paid work themselves. Out of all the successful part-time workers, only a lucky few will ever find a full-time position for a pyrotechnic company, or perhaps eventually start their own business.

Pyrotechnicians who want to do pyrotechnic special effects follow a similar career path, volunteering and training with experienced pyrotechnicians for years before receiving even part-time work. Almost all pyrotechnicians who make a career out of film production and special effects work in Hollywood, and people interested in this type of pyrotechnics will most likely need to relocate to Los Angeles to find someone to train with. After training and some work experience, pyrotechnicians who work with special effects can either start their own businesses, freelance, or work full time for a special effects company, a traveling stunt show, or a theme park that puts on stunt shows.

Pitfalls

Pyrotechnics is a small, competitive field that rarely pays well, except for managers or the few top pyrotechnicians in movies who may earn enough to quit their day job.

Pyrotechnicians accept the drawbacks for one reason: They love creating art out

Brandon Merrill, pyrotechnician

For New Hampshire fireworks aficionado Brandon Merrill, fireworks are in his blood: He became interested in the job as a result of his brother Brett's involvement in the field.

"I get a certain thrill while shooting," Merrill explains. "I always enjoyed watching fireworks, and there's an actual thrill with shooting the stuff." Although shooting fireworks usually entails long, hot hours on the job, it's worth it, Merrill says. In a typical fireworks display valued at $7,000, there may be 700 shots (not including the 1,000 to 1,500 shots for the grand finale). If the shots are lit by flares (and not by electrical devices), that means Merrill must light each wick with a flare—by hand. "Most people don't realize the amount of work and the space you need to set off a show like that," Merrill explained.

"The first few I did were small shows, with small shells," Merrill explains. The bigger shells, which can be up to eight inches across, are considerably more dangerous. "If there's going to be a problem," Merrill explains, "it's probably with larger fireworks, because of the lift charge. In an 8-inch shell, there's a lot of explosives."

Although the risk is minimal, he says, there are occasionally serious accidents—usually with these bigger explosives. But, he stresses, given the large number of shows and the amount of fireworks, there are relatively very few accidents. Typically, Merrill says he hears of only a couple of accidents throughout New England in any one year. Fatal accidents almost never occur.

of fire. In fact, there are many people who do pyrotechnics as a hobby. Those who want to be professional pyrotechnicians must be passionate enough about the work to spend years volunteering on Fourth of July fireworks shows or working for little to no pay on pyrotechnic special effects in films and stunt shows before receiving their first paid job.

Moreover, fireworks involve danger and unpredictability—those rare times when something goes wrong, or doesn't go at all.

Perks

For the very few extremely successful pyrotechnicians who build large businesses, salaries can be quite high and the work is creative and always new. For the rest of those who just love fireworks, the job is creative, exciting, and thrilling.

Get a Jump on the Job

You can't actually work as an apprentice until you're 21, but you can get a head start by working hard in school on physics and chemistry. Those who want to work in pyrotechnic stunts or special effects should also take lots of art and music classes.

RODEO CLOWN

OVERVIEW

Being voted class clown is one thing, but using your talents to try and entertain, amuse, and ultimately distract an angry 2,000-pound bull is quite another. But that's exactly what rodeo clowns do every time they go to work.

There are two basic types of rodeo clowns—the barrelman and the bullfighter. Barrelmen stay near (or even inside) a specially constructed barrel in the middle of the arena during the bull-riding competition. The barrel, also known as the "clown lounge," was invented by a barrelman named Jasbo. Made out of heavy-gauge steel and lined with industrial foam rubber, it weighs 175 pounds—sturdy enough to protect the barrelman and give bull riders a safe place to go if they're bucked off in the middle of the arena. After an event, the barrelman will spend up to an hour using a five-pound mallet to pound dents out of the barrel.

Bullfighters, on the other hand, wait for the rider to be bucked off. Then it's their turn to take center stage, distracting the bull so that the rider can escape. The bullfighter is actually in the ring during the ride, staying within 10 to 15 feet of the bull so he can step in the moment the rider is bucked off. The bullfighter helps the rider get a feel for the bull, helping the rider to work the bull and ultimately earn a higher score. The bullfighter also might be called on to distract the bull when the rider dismounts after completing a successful eight-second ride.

Fans love the bullfighters so much that bullfighting has even become a

AT A GLANCE

Salary Range
Rodeo clowns negotiate their own contracts with the stock contractors or the rodeo committee. For small, local, or regional rodeos, they might make $100 to $250, to cover their expenses. Once they have made a name for themselves, bullfighters can make $500 or more per performance, and barrelmen can make $400 to $1,200 or more per performance.

Education/Experience
None required, but most attend a school or camp to learn the tricks of the trade.

Personal Attributes
Should have quick reflexes and be physically fit with a strong mental attitude. Should be concerned with the welfare and safety of others and able to put up with pain. Should have a strong desire to become a rodeo clown along with the physical ability to do the job and be creative, energetic, and funny.

Requirements
Many of the top rodeo and bull-riding organizations require you to become a member in order to work their events. You generally need to be 18 years old (or the age of majority in your state) to apply for membership. Other events might require you to be 18 years old because of liability issues.

Outlook
With the popularity of rodeos and bull riding on the rise, there may be opportunities for talented, hardworking rodeo clowns.

rodeo event of its own. During the competition, it's man against beast, one-on-one, where the bullfighter spends at least 40 seconds in the arena with a rider-less Spanish bull. An additional 30 seconds is optional. The bullfighter can call the match at any time after the required 40 seconds. Points are given for

Jerry Norton, bullfighter and rodeo clown

The tenacity of a middle linebacker, with the speed of a sprinter and the moves of a running back, is what it takes to be a bullfighter/rodeo clown, according to Jerry Norton. And if anyone should know, it's Norton, a 1998 World Champion Bullfighter. "You also need to be able to handle pain," says Norton, speaking from experience. He's had a broken jaw, reconstructed knee, shoulder surgery, and countless other minor injuries.

Norton started down the path to his rodeo career by getting involved with 4-H and youth rodeos as a youngster. "I always watched the bullfighters," he recalls. "It looked fun, but challenging. It gets in your blood, and it's hard to leave alone." He admits that while getting to travel to different parts of the country is one of the best parts of his job, being away from his family is tough. Still, he's content.

"I feel lucky at a young age to have found something I like to do," he says, "and that I can make a living at."

The hardest part of the job is to override your natural instinct to get out of the way. As for the bulls in the ring, Norton says you need a certain amount of fear, but you also need to respect the bulls.

"The bulls play for keeps!" Norton reminds young enthusiasts. To aspiring rodeo clowns, he advises: "Go to a good, reputable school, and don't try this at home."

how the fighter moves around the bull, the different moves the fighter makes, how close the bull gets to the fighter, and the number of risks the fighter takes during the match.

Both barrelmen and bullfighters are responsible for keeping the bull rider safe. And while the work of the barrelman isn't as dangerous as that of a bullfighter, it's actually a more important job. In addition to "working the barrel," the barrelman is responsible for amusing the crowd between riders or events (or during commercial breaks at an event being televised). The barrelman also has to be ready to take over during any unexpected delay during the rodeo—in the event of an injury, if an uncooperative bull won't leave the chute, or anything else. The barrelman might perform skits, use props, joke with the announcers, or even call on a few audience members for "assistance." Because of these extra duties, barrelmen are paid more than the bullfighters.

Because these jobs are risky, both barrelmen and bullfighters wear protective equipment under their clown clothes. Still, injuries can happen. The question isn't *if* a barrelman or bullfighter will be injured, it's *when* and how badly. Over the course of a career, these rodeo experts suffer multiple injuries—bumps, bruises, concussions, broken bones, and worse.

If you decide that you want to take on the bull, you'll want to get some training and experience first. Many rodeo clowns get their training apprenticing under more experienced clowns at small local and regional rodeos, and at youth rodeo events. Many also attend a rodeo clown training school or camp where you'll work with bulls that aren't as strong or as mean as those used for events. In addition to learning ways to help you stay safe in the arena, you might learn how to put on your clown face, how to put together a costume, and a variety of techniques for entertaining the audience.

Most rodeo clowns work toward membership in large rodeo associations such as the Professional Rodeo Cowboys Association (PRCA). However, membership isn't automatic; clowns and other specialty acts must be able to show tapes of some performances at events before earning a membership. It's not the sort of sport for older people; when your clowning days are done, you might stay involved by working as an announcer at rodeo events, or training the next generation of bullfighters and barrelmen.

Pitfalls

The risk of injury and the severity of those injuries is the biggest pitfall in this career. Moreover, many bullfighters and barrelmen have to work other full-time jobs, saving their rodeo work for the weekends—until they hit it big.

Perks

You'll get the best seat in the house during the bull-riding events, and you'll get to be a part of one of the most popular spectator sports in the country. You'll also be responsible for saving the lives of bull riders, which can be a pretty nice feeling.

Get a Jump on the Job

You can start learning traditional clown skills—makeup, skits, gags, and working with props—at any age. Those talents will help you when you are entertaining the crowd. There are several rodeo organizations for students under 18. Contact the American Junior Rodeo Association (http://www.ajra.org), the National High School Rodeo Association (www.nhsra.org), or the National Little Britches Rodeo Association (http://www.nlbra.com) for opportunities to get some experience clowning around.

SECRET SERVICE AGENT

OVERVIEW

You've probably seen them on TV whenever the president or a foreign head of state appears—the serious fellows in the suits, eyes shielded by sunglasses, microphone in their ear, scanning the crowds.

Secret Service agents make up the branch of law enforcement charged with both protecting the world's leaders and the U.S. financial system. Most people think of "protection" when they think of a secret service agent, but in fact, the agency was established in 1865 solely to suppress the counterfeiting of U.S. currency. At the time, experts estimated more than half the circulating currency was fake. Over the years, the agency's investigative responsibilities have expanded to include investigating counterfeiting of currency and securities, forgery and altering government checks and bonds, thefts and fraud relating to electronic funds transfer, financial access device fraud, identity fraud, telecommunications fraud, computer fraud, telemarketing fraud, and fraud concerning federally insured financial institutions. The Secret Service is a federal law enforcement agency, but they don't gather intelligence like the CIA. Agents do work undercover during their criminal investigations.

In 1901, following the assassination of President William McKinley in Buffalo, the Secret Service was assigned the responsibility of protecting the president. Today, agents are required to protect the president and vice president of the United

States and their immediate families; former presidents and their spouses, widows, and children (to age 16);

major presidential and vice presidential candidates and their spouses; and visiting foreign heads of state. They're also obliged to protect anyone else authorized by the president. In 1997, congressional legislation became effective limiting Secret Service protection to former presidents for a period of not more than 10 years from the date the president leaves office.

For example, when the president is at the White House, the Secret Service Uniformed Division, the Metropolitan Police Department, and the U.S. Park Police patrol the streets and parks nearby. The Secret Service Technical Security Division regularly consults with experts from other agencies. The military supports the Secret Service through the use of bomb experts and communications resources. When the president travels, an advance team of Secret Service agents works with the host city and state law enforcement and public safety officials to protect him.

If you join the Secret Service, you'll be working out of either their headquarters in Washington, D.C., or one of more than 125 offices throughout the United States and abroad. The Secret Service employs about 2,100 special agents, 1,200 Uniformed Division officers, and approximately 1,700 other technical, professional, and administrative support personnel.

The Secret Service Uniformed Division is a uniformed force whose members protect the White House Complex, the vice president's residence, and foreign embassies and missions in the Washington, D.C. area. You'll see them standing guard at the White House gates, the main Treasury building and annex, other presidential offices, the vice president's residence, and at embassies, protecting these buildings as well as the people in them.

Members of the Secret Service Countersniper Team (you might see them on top of the White House) include specially trained Uniformed Division officers whose mission is to neutralize any long-range threat to the president or any of the other leaders or family members they protect.

Members of the Uniformed Division also perform other missions in support of the protection of the president, such as operating magnetometers, or acting as countersnipers, canine handlers, or at special operations posts.

If you wanted to pursue a career as an agent, you'd start by getting an intensive 10 weeks of training at the Federal Law Enforcement Training Center in Glynco, Georgia, designed to train new federal investigators in such areas as criminal law and investigative techniques. It provides a general foundation for the agency-specific training to follow—an 11-week Special Agent Training Course at a Secret Service training facility in Beltsville, Maryland, for advanced training in basic knowledge and advanced application training in combating counterfeiting, access device fraud and other financial criminal activity, protective intelligence investigations, physical protection techniques, protective advances and emergency medicine. You'll also get extensive training in firearms, control tactics, water survival skills, and physical fitness.

The Secret Agent school is only attended by Secret Service agents and officers; but even after agents or officers have completed both schools, they continue to receive training throughout their careers. You'll regularly get specialized training, including regular firearms requalifications and emergency medicine refreshers. Detail agents also participate in unique simulated crisis training scenarios called

David Stenhouse, former Secret Service agent

For former state trooper David Stenhouse, being able to see the world while protecting the president was a strong incentive to start training for an elite position as a Secret Service agent. "Being a trooper gave me a good foundation," he says, but he had to start all over to be trained as an agent. After his training, he spent his first few years investigating financial crimes.

"Basically, agents spend a lot more time on the investigating duties than protecting duties," he says. After about five years in the Seattle office, he was pulled off to begin protecting. For example, he'd be suddenly sent to San Diego to protect the president who was in town for the day. Another time, he was sent to Guam to protect the President of Micronesia, who was visiting. In the past, Stenhouse has protected former Presidents Bill Clinton, Jimmy Carter, and George H. W. Bush, and current President George W. Bush. He's also protected presidential families: former First Ladies Barbara Bush and Hillary Clinton, former First Child Chelsea Clinton, and other heads of state, including the president of Iceland and the prime minister of Albania. He doesn't have lots of stories about personal interactions, however. "You can't be talking to the president," he explains, "because if you're talking to him, you're not looking away into the crowd for threats, which is what you're supposed to be doing. Of course, if he speaks to you, you answer!"

In the course of his career as an agent, Stenhouse traveled to Israel, Europe, Japan, and Guam. "I traveled all around," he says. "It was a great opportunity. After four years, I'd been to 34 of the 50 states on business."

But the job did have its downside. "There were 18- to 20-hour days," he says. "I'd go three to four weeks without a day off. You might come back from Japan one day on an investigation, and have to go out on protection the next day. It's not a job for someone who wants to settle down and raise a family." For that reason, Stenhouse retired from the service to work as a cybersleuth and be able to spend more time with his family. But he has fond memories of the important job he did as an agent. "You're carrying a gun for a reason," he says. "You have people out there who want to harm you, or harm the president. You're trained to fight."

"AOP" or Attack on Principal. These exercises present agents with a variety of "real world" emergency situations involving Secret Service protectees and are designed to provide agents with immediate feedback concerning their response to the problems.

Once you are trained, you spend four or five years in a field office doing investigations into crimes such as credit card fraud, computer fraud, bank fraud, and counterfeiting. Even though you'd rely on computers to help, you'd still go out and questions victims, witnesses, and suspects. After the field office assignments,

you'd be transferred to a protective detail, where you would stay for another three to five years investigating people who make threats against political leaders.

Most agents don't have to wear a uniform—just a business suit. They're not required to wear sunglasses, but most do to keep the sun out of their eyes and to prohibit people from knowing where they're looking. That swirled wire you might have seen around their ear is attached to a special radio that allows agents to talk privately with other agents. Agents have a piece of equipment called a surveillance kit, containing a microphone and an earpiece connected to a radio. Having a microphone lets them hang a radio on their belt so that they can keep their hands free while they are working—which is very important when you're protecting someone.

Agents also carry guns—the Sig Sauer P229, 357 caliber pistol. They also are trained on the Remington Model 870 shotgun, the Uzi submachine gun, and the MP5 automatic weapon. They also are issued bullet-resistant vests.

Pitfalls

The hours can be killer—sometimes as much as 20 hours a day—and you may go for a month without a day off. This job is great for an energetic, healthy younger person, but someone interested in spending lots of quality time with a family will have major problems. You also must keep in mind that this can be a dangerous job—Secret Service agents are prepared to give their life for the protection of the president. As of 2003, 34 Secret Service employees have died as a result of on-duty incidents.

Perks

You'll certainly have an exciting life as a Secret Service agent—there is tons of international and national travel, and you get to be quite close to top international leaders.

Get a Jump on the Job

If you think you'd like to try for a job as a Secret Service agent, you can start right now by getting top grades and avoiding getting into trouble—no drinking, smoking, or drugs—because there are stringent background checks that go back all the way back into your childhood. Try to be the best person you can be.

SKI PATROLLER

OVERVIEW

Do you love the outdoors, love to ski, and love to help others and do emergency rescue work? Would you like to have a job with a bit of mystique? Would you like to ski for up to nine hours a day, five days a week?

If you answered "yes" to these questions—and you think you've got what it takes to wear the red ski jacket with a white cross—then you might want to consider a career in the ski patrol. Ski patrolling isn't for everybody, but for some, it's the best job in the world.

As a ski patroller, your duties may include watching out for avalanches, maintaining trails, and keeping track of weather data.

Unfortunately, the biggest part of a ski patrollers' job is to take care of injuries that occur on the slopes. If someone gets hurt, ski patrollers contact emergency medical services and rescue injured skiers. They may need to perform CPR, administer first aid, work with rescue dogs, and perform lift evacuations, avalanche rescue, and high angle rescues.

Since taking care of emergencies is such a big part of the job, patrollers must keep a constant eye out for skiers, patrolling trails and slopes on foot, or watching from a tower. You may need to pick up a pair of binoculars to detect hazards, disturbances, or identify safety infractions, and be able to warn skiers about bad weather, unsafe areas, or illegal conduct.

Then there's the hardware part of the job—at many ski areas, ski patrollers sometimes must inspect equipment such as rope tows, T-bar, J-bar, and chair lifts,

AT A GLANCE

Salary Range

Wages vary by location, employer, type of work, and experience, training, and responsibility, but typically begin at about $9 an hour.

Education/Experience

High school diploma, excellent skiing ability. Experience as a ski instructor or ski patrol volunteer is helpful for ski patrol jobs.

Personal Attributes

Good people skills, physical fitness, service orientation.

Requirements

Most ski patrollers must be 21 with a valid driver's license. CPR certification and/or EMT certification is usually required. To become a certified member of the Professional Ski Patrol Association, candidates must pass each of four exams: Ski/Snowboard, Toboggan, First Aid, and a written exam. Each candidate must attend and successfully complete a pre-course in order to qualify for the exam. The American Red Cross and the American Heart Association also certify protective service workers in CPR. Courses for emergency response professionals require up to 67 hours of training; more than half of those focus on emergency response. Ski patrollers who also teach may need emergency response certification.

Outlook

Fair. Ski patroller jobs are extremely competitive; smaller mountains may use volunteer patrols. Best chance for a full-time career is in the larger ski resorts in western United States.

checking for safety hazards and damage or wear. If that isn't enough balls to juggle, many ski patrollers also teach skiing in their spare time.

Of course, skiing is the most important part of the job. You've got to be

Julie Rust, ski patroller

The beauty of the job," explains Julie Rust, director of the Vail Ski Patrol, "is that no job is typical." She punches in, goes to the morning meeting, and then it's out to check trails, mark downed trees, and do avalanche checks. Then it's time to check the public and take care of the injuries. "For an EMT, once the ambulance gets there, the patient is taken care of," Rust says. "Here, once we get the person on the toboggan, it's still 10 degrees in the middle of the forest. For big mountains, extrication and evacuation is critically important."

A ski patroller for the past 20 years, one of the things Rust likes best about the job is the amount of time she can spend skiing. "I'd worked several jobs in the ski areas," she recalls, "but the ski patrol looked like the most challenging. You may think, when you go out the door, that you're going out to do one thing," she says, "but then there's a medical emergency and suddenly you're doing something completely different."

able to ski comfortably anywhere and everywhere—you should be a solid skier who can ski with heavy backpacks, tools, and toboggans. Skiing has to be second nature.

Ski patrollers learn the many skills they need in a variety of training programs, which usually lead to ski patroller certification. These programs teach methods of emergency rescue, first aid, and how to spot danger on the slopes and prevent injuries and accidents.

Once you've been trained, you'll be screened by the mountain in charge of hiring for the ski patrol. Often, this process includes ski tests—rigorous examinations of an applicant's skiing ability on terrain ranging from wide-open ski slopes to double-diamond mogul runs. You have to be a strong, solid skier, because it's important in getting to somebody who's injured down the mountain. At smaller mountains, passing the ski test is all that's required. At larger mountains, such as Vail, skiers who pass the ski test then attend the mountain's ski patrol academy—a four-day program of instruction on rescue toboggans, rope systems, high-angle and avalanche rescues, first aid, chairlift evacuations, and accident scene management. At the end of the four days, students fill out job applications, take preliminary interviews, and hope they'll be asked to join the team come next ski season.

While there is a certain mystique about the job, working on the ski patrol is far from glamorous. Patrollers must get on the mountain early in frigid conditions, to haul equipment, string ropes, bring loaded toboggans down the mountain and pack snow.

It's fun, but it's a lot of work too. On powder days, you're out doing avalanche control. There are trails to check, obstacles to mark, skiers to watch. You may also get calls to take people down the mountain because they've been hurt.

Pitfalls

Ski patrol jobs are seasonal in all areas of the country, so most ski patrollers have other jobs during the off-season. You won't get rich doing this job, and many positions don't include benefits because it's considered seasonal employment.

Perks

If you love the outdoors and love skiing, then being a ski patroller can be an ideal way to combine the two—and you're actually getting paid to ski more than 100 days a season. Add in the extra benefit of helping others and sharing your love of skiing, and many patrollers swear their profession is the best.

Get a Jump on the Job

The best way to prepare for a job as a ski patroller is to get out there and start skiing—have fun, but follow the rules. Join the ski club or ski team at your school, if there is one. Teach skiing at your local mountain. Take first aid courses or CPR as soon as they're offered in your community.

SMOKEJUMPER

OVERVIEW

The call comes in: *Wildland fire in the backwoods!* Within 10 minutes, a team of jumpers gets suited up and on a plane, flying low over a heavily wooded area totally engulfed in flames, ready to jump out into the midst of chaos. That's the start of another work shift for smokejumpers.

Since 1940, smokejumpers have been the first ones on the scene of wildland fires in remote areas, famous for getting into places conventional firefighters and fire-fighting equipment could never reach. They can be at the scene of any fire within 100 miles of their base in about 30 minutes.

Once the plane reaches the fire, it circles the area while the jumpers survey the fire, the area, and the conditions and make decisions about the best way to fight the fire. Before leaving the plane, a spotter drops weighted papers and streamers to determine the speed and direction of the wind. The spotter remains on board the plane, giving the pilot and jumpers information about the wind, the fire, and the terrain. After the smokejumpers have landed, their supplies (contained in a *fire box*) are dropped in by parachute. The fire box includes enough tools, food, and water for two people for up to 48 hours. One fire box is dropped for each pair of smokejumpers on the scene.

Smokejumpers wear a padded kevlar jumpsuit to protect them from the fire and from the trees, rocks, and other dangers they'll encounter during the jump. They also wear a helmet with a metal face grate. When they jump from the plane, each smokejumper carries an extra 80 pounds of clothes and equipment.

Once the fire is out, smokejumpers pack up their equipment and lug it to the closest road or helicopter landing pad. Their packs can weight up to 110 pounds, and they may have to carry it as far as 10 miles or more in rough terrain.

There are about 400 smokejumpers in the United States who work for two agencies, the Bureau of Land Management (BLM) and the Forest Service (FS), traveling all around the country to help fight wildland blazes. BLM smokejumpers are stationed at bases in Fairbanks, Arkansas, and Boise,

AT A GLANCE

Salary Range

$10 an hour to start; base managers make $35+ an hour.

Education/Experience

At least a high school diploma.

Personal Attributes

Team and organizational skills, leadership potential, good communication skills, ability to work well under extreme pressure and stress and make decisions in any situation.

Requirements

Applicants must have one year of general experience (forestry, agricultural, or range work, or related college courses) and one to three seasons' experience fighting wildland fires, or equivalent skills and knowledge. Must be in excellent physical condition, and meet height, weight, hearing, vision, and health requirements.

Outlook

Competition for smokejumping jobs is stiff. Each job listing receives many applications from qualified applicants.

Mike Tupper, smokejumper

Persistence definitely paid off for smokejumper Mike Tupper. After high school, he became a successful real estate agent in Las Vegas and spent some time running one of the largest mortgage companies in Nevada. However, he was unhappy with his job and looking for something fun to do.

"When I found out that they actually paid people to fight fires," Tupper recalls, "I went to the Las Vegas Fire Department every week until they told me that they'd hire me if I promised not to come back until my start date." His first summer on the job, he met some of the Alaska smokejumpers and decided this was for him. He applied from 1981 until 1984, when he was finally hired as a member of the Alaska Hot Shot crew. Again, persistence paid off. The next year Tupper was offered a job as a smokejumper.

Today, Tupper is a member of Nevada's Great Basin Smokejumpers, and among his duties is the recruiting, hiring, and training of new smokejumpers. "We get 10 to 30 applications for each vacancy. We want [to hire] the best all-around person." Although some of the skills can be taught, Tupper says, smokejumpers really need to have the attitude and work ethic, along with a good fire background. They also look for leadership potential—someone who can take charge as needed. It's also a physically demanding career. "Smokejumping is very hard on your body," Tupper says, who counts a broken jaw and broken ankle among his injuries.

His best advice for someone interested in the job? "Go to school and get a degree in case you need something to fall back on," he says, adding that a degree in biological science is the best choice if you want to stay involved with a fire management program. But most important, Tupper says: "Do your best at everything, every day."

Idaho, whereas FS smokejumpers work out of Winthrop, Washington; Grangeville and McCall, Idaho; Missoula and West Yellowstone, Minnesota; Redmond, Oregon; and Redding, California.

Even when they aren't fighting fires, smokejumpers keep busy piling brush and doing prescribed burning of very dry brush in a controlled situation before it can become fuel for a fire. Smokejumpers also work on upkeep at their base facilities and doing trail maintenance, and travel around the country evaluating state and local fire plans.

If you want to become a smokejumper, you've got to get some experience fighting wildland fires, because smokejumpers fight fires in very harsh environments and steep terrain, with extreme temperatures, high altitudes, and lots of smoke.

As a smokejumping applicant, you'll need to be able to do seven pull-ups, 25 push-ups, 45 sit-ups, run 1.5 miles in less than 11 minutes, and complete a pack test (also called a work capacity test) where you carry 110 pounds over a three-mile flat course. If you're still breathing after all of that physical stress, you're eligible to enter the smokejumper training program held each spring, before fire season starts (from about June 1 through October 31).

The four-week training program starts with about 20 hours of classroom training before the hands-on training begins. Out of the classroom, you'll do parachute training (including parachute jumps). You'll learn how to use and maintain the tools of the trade, including pumps and chainsaws. You'll learn how to climb trees and how to safely land in water. After finishing your training, you'll spend several weeks in Alaska fighting fires before you return to your home base.

Experienced returning smokejumpers also go through training each spring, and veterans are required to successfully complete another physical test before returning to the program. After passing the test, veterans receive refresher training in parachuting, tree-climbing, and fire-fighting techniques. Also as a part of their training program, veteran jumpers develop a daily physical training program that includes running, push-ups, sit-ups, and pull-ups.

Some smokejumpers also are trained as emergency medical technicians (EMTs); those jumpers update their training each spring.

Pitfalls

There are only nine smokejumper bases in the United States, so if you want to do this job you may have to relocate, at least during fire season. But the biggest pitfall is the risk. Any job fighting fires is dangerous, but smokejumpers have more than the fire to worry about—it can be dangerous to parachute into a fire. Amazingly, there have only been three parachute-related deaths in the more than 130,000 jumps since the program began. Wildland fires also can be unpredictable. Many times jumpers end up battling the elements as well as the fire; a sudden change in wind direction can trap them in the middle of a blaze.

Perks

The brotherhood of smokejumpers is very strong, and all jumpers understand theirs is vital, important work. Not only do they work to save the country's natural resources, but by working to stop wildland fires before they get out of control, they also save countless lives.

Get a Jump on the Job

Since you're required to have experience fighting wildland fires before you can begin smokejumper training, look for places and ways to get that experience. Smokejumping is a very physically demanding job. Consider starting a training program to get in shape to meet the requirements of the physical test required before training, and to meet the demands of the job.

STEEPLEJACK

OVERVIEW

A steeplejack is someone who builds, inspects, maintains, repairs, or restores tall structures such as church steeples, clock towers, chimneys, and high-rise buildings. If you do an Internet search for more information on becoming a steeplejack, you will find many training programs and apprenticeships in Europe. And, while those same programs and apprenticeships aren't available in the United States, that doesn't mean that there aren't ample opportunities for individuals interested in becoming a steeplejack.

If you become a steeplejack, you'll be performing ordinary tasks at extraordinary heights, often 50 to 500 feet above the ground. Of course, you'll start out a lot closer to the ground, maybe even on the ground, performing minor repairs. Since you'll be learning the skill of the trade while you are working on the job, your training may be a little bit different from that of other steeplejacks.

During your training, you'll work under the watchful eye of a supervisor. You'll learn the standard practices and processes of the steeplejack trade. You'll learn how to correctly and safely use the various tools, materials, and equipment on the job site. You'll learn to read and work from project specifications and blueprints. You'll learn how to properly rig scaffolds, platforms, ladders, bosun's seats (harnesses), and other equipment. And, as your training progresses, you'll learn how to climb high structures and work at unusual heights. You might even choose to specialize in a particular type of repair work or a specific restoration process.

AT A GLANCE

Salary Range

Varies among employers, starting at minimum wage and going up. Pay is not always based on skills; it depends more on the height of the project and the height at which you work.

Education/Experience

None required, but employers or training programs may want you to have a high school diploma.

Personal Attributes

Safety-conscious. Willing to work at unusual heights (50 to 500 feet or higher). Physically fit. Sure-footed, with good coordination and a good sense of balance.

Requirements

Able to climb ladders and move heavy objects. Some states require steeplejacks to be licensed contractors.

Outlook

As the country's early churches, first high-rise buildings, towers, and other structures age, they will need restoration services, which means work for steeplejacks. Steeplejacks may also be called into service to work on the maintenance of current high-rises.

As a steeplejack, you'll spend your days working on any number of tall structures such as church steeples and spires, smokestacks, towers, cupolas, chimneys, flagpoles, clock towers, and monuments. You'll inspect these structures for safety and to evaluate problem areas that need repair. You'll also maintain, repair, and restore these structures. You might restore masonry or stonework. You might also install, replace, or remove lightening rods, weathervanes, flagpoles, aviation lights, or antennas. If your client has a problem with birds, you might be hired to clean up and bird-proof an area. You will perform

Nick America, steeplejack

"I get to go places very few other people ever get to go," says steeplejack Nick America, whose work often finds him high off the ground—about 250 feet up if he's working on a church steeple, or as much as 1,000 to 1,500 feet off the ground if he's working on a tower. As with many of today's steeplejacks, it is a profession that has been passed down through the generations.

America's great-grandfather was a steeplejack in Ireland. When he immigrated to the United States, he continued to work in the trade. Although his family did get out of the business for a while, he reopened Steeplejacks of America in 1968 because of the demand for the quality work the company was known for doing. America's son and grandson are carrying on the family tradition.

"Not a lot of people do it," America explains. "Each beautiful steeple gives you a new challenge." As master mechanics, steeplejacks "can go to anyplace and do whatever needs to be done to repair the project."

Surprisingly, America is somewhat casual about the heights at which he's required to work, claiming that once you're strapped in securely, there's really nothing to it. One of the most unique challenges America has faced was working on the gold rooster that sits atop the Pittsburgh Theological Seminary—a monster rooster, six feet wide and four to five feet tall. The wind had broken the tail on the rooster, which had to be removed, repaired, and then replaced.

"You may not want to do it forever," America says, "but it's a good experience for the young. Start with painting or roof work, and don't be afraid to work at heights."

routine maintenance such as cleaning, sandblasting, stripping, painting, patching, caulking, and waterproofing. You might also preserve and restore historic structures: cleaning them, repairing or replacing gold leaf or gilding, repairing or replacing glass, doing façade work, or doing clock repair. Some steeplejacks are even hired to install and remove banners, holiday decorations, and displays.

As a steeplejack, you'll probably work for a business or company that specializes in steeplejack services. The jobs and tasks you do will depend in part on your company's specialties and the needs of your clients. If you work as a steeplejack in this type of job, you'll probably have to travel at least occasionally for your job. Some universities hire steeplejacks to maintain their buildings. State and local governments also employ steeplejacks to maintain and repair government-owned

buildings, radio and television towers, and bridges.

Whatever you do, no two jobs will be the same. In fact, sometimes you'll be called on to perform some rather unusual tasks. In 2000, a steeplejack at the University of California at Berkeley was called upon to scale the 307-foot Sather Tower, known as the Campanile, to retrieve a large pumpkin. It wasn't the first time that steeplejacks had to climb the tower to remove pranksters' "additions." A Mickey Mouse face once appeared on the face of the clock, complete with giant white gloves on the hands of the clock.

Pitfalls

Like many construction-related jobs, the work can be dirty. Steeplejacks often have to deal with an added mess—bird guano. Depending on your location the work is often seasonal, and you often have to work in adverse weather conditions to get a job done on schedule. Much of the work is on the east coast of the United States, which might mean relocating, or traveling to and staying at a worksite for an extended period of time.

Perks

Steeplejacks get a great bird's-eye view of the area they are working in. With all the climbing up and down ladders, steeplejacks stay in great shape.

Get a Jump on the Job

Take advantage of classes, jobs, and other experiences where you can learn basic construction skills. Learn how to correctly and safely operate hand and power tools. If possible, check out a rappelling clinic or other opportunities to make sure that you enjoy it and working off the ground won't be a problem for you.

TEXAS RANGER

OVERVIEW

The Texas Rangers are the oldest law enforcement organization in North America, and they've been protecting the people of Texas since 1823. As living symbols of a unique heritage, you'll see them wearing the boots, white hats, and pistol belts from long ago, but as elite law enforcement officers of the 21st century, they've added college degrees, networked computers, cell phones, and state-of-the-art forensic analyses.

The Rangers are part of the history of the Old West, from the shoot-from-the hip tradition of independent lawmen. In 1821, Stephen F. Austin brought 300 families to the Spanish province of Texas, where it was quickly apparent that—with criminals running amok—something needed to be done. That something was a group of men called "Rangers" that Austin organized in 1823 to provide protection. He came up with the name because the men had to "range" over the entire country. Since then, the Ranger Service has differed in organization and policy under varying conditions, demands for service, and state administrations, and it has not been of entirely unbroken continuity. When the Texas legislature created the Texas Department of Public Safety in 1935, the Texas Rangers became part of this agency, with statewide law enforcement jurisdiction.

Today, the Texas Rangers focus on major felony cases and major crimes, conducting criminal and special investigations, arresting criminals, suppressing riots, and helping local law enforcement officials as the investigative division of the Texas Department of Public Safety. The 118 Rangers are posted across Texas in six companies headquartered in Waco, Houston, Midland, Garland (the Dallas-Ft. Worth metroplex), Lubbock, and San Antonio, with an administrative office in Austin. An unsolved crimes investigative team is located in San Antonio.

You have to work as a deputy for at least eight years and spend time on highway patrol, motor vehicle theft, and narcotics before you're even eligible to apply for

---

AT A GLANCE

Salary Range

$40,345 to $80,000.

Education/Experience

A minimum of 90 semester hours from an accredited college plus eight years of law enforcement experience and current employment with the Texas Department of Public Safety as commissioned officer with the rank of at least Trooper II; 36 months or more military or law enforcement experience may be substituted for required semester hours.

Personal Attributes

Courage, tenacity, good people skills, solid work ethic, interest in justice.

Requirements

U.S. citizenship, excellent health, minimum age 20, valid Texas driver's license, background check. Applicants also must pass an entrance exam; those with the highest grades will appear before an Oral Interview Board for final selection.

Outlook

Difficult. Since there are only 118 Rangers, competition is fierce. There are usually between 40 and 200 applicants for every position.

Lt. George Turner, Texas Ranger

Ilike the freedom," explains Lt. George Turner of Company F in the Texas Rangers. In a state the size of Texas, Turner has 44 counties to patrol, in 100 square miles of Texas sagebrush. Why else does he like his job? "I think there's a mystique about it."

Turner always wanted to be in law enforcement, he says, and he knew he wanted to try for the best—the job of Texas Ranger. As a lieutenant, he's assigned to a desk now, but his favorite part of the job is still "dealing out some justice" to the bad guys he comes across. The hardest part of his job, he says, is handling the crimes where children are the victims.

a Ranger job. Because it takes superior credentials to become a Texas Ranger, ranks begin with sergeant, followed by lieutenant, captain, and chief (or senior captain). While the Ranger position is open to women, there aren't a lot of them in the force. There are currently two female Texas Rangers; officially, the first female Rangers were appointed in 1993.

Pitfalls

The job of a Texas Ranger can be stressful and dangerous, involve long hours and plenty of hard work, and carries some of the same pitfalls as any type of police work—it can be difficult dealing with criminals and seeing firsthand some of the pain and tragedy caused by crime.

Perks

Aside from the simple prestige that being a Ranger entails, the job appeals to the independent Texas spirit that allows its Rangers extraordinary freedom to do the job as they see fit.

Get a Jump on the Job

If you want to be a Texas Ranger, stay in school, become familiar with the law enforcement skills and technology of the 21st century, build a solid record of service, and join the Texas Department of Public Safety.

You also can become a Junior Texas Ranger through a special program of the Texas Ranger Hall of Fame and Museum. This nonprofit program supports the renovation and improvement of the museum and its educational programs. Joining the Junior Rangers includes an appointment certificate from the Texas Ranger Hall of Fame signed by an active-duty Texas Ranger, two junior Ranger toy badges, a family ticket for four to the Texas Ranger Hall of Fame and Museum in Waco, and inscription in the Junior Ranger Hall of Fame and Museum membership roll.

VOLCANOLOGIST

OVERVIEW

Picture how the history of Pompeii might be different if they'd had a volcanologist around who could have predicted the eruption of Mt. Vesuvius. That's about how valuable these adventuresome scientists are today.

As a volcanologist, one of your jobs would be to collect and analyze data about volcanoes so that you can predict when a volcano is going erupt. And that's a pretty important job. If you say that a volcano is going to erupt and it doesn't, then people have spent time and money evacuating their homes and businesses for no reason. If you don't predict an eruption, or you say a volcano isn't going to erupt and it does, then people will be injured and killed.

Predicting eruption is an important part of what volcanologists do, but it's not the only thing. They study many different things about volcanoes. Some volcanologists study volcanoes as possible sources of energy and minerals. Others map the changes in the lava flow field. Some collect data and use it to locate ore deposits so they can tell miners where to look. Some volcanologists study earthquakes in volcanoes, while others study specific types of eruptions.

To become a volcanologist takes a lot of time and school. After high school, you need to go to college—but because very few colleges offer undergraduate degrees in volcanology, you'll need to major in geography, where you'll learn the basics you need you'll need for graduate school. You'll take classes in geophysics, geochemistry, petrology, structural geology, sedimentary geology, and remote sensing.

AT A GLANCE

Salary Range
Technician positions (with a bachelor's degree) start around $25,000. Volcanologists with a Ph.D. generally start around $40,000; with experience, they can earn $100,000 or more per year.

Education/Experience
Doctorate in geology.

Personal Attributes
Need to like science and enjoy working outdoors.

Requirements
None.

Outlook
There are about 200 volcanologists in the United States, most of whom work for the U.S. Geological Survey (USGS). As a government-funded agency, the USGS often feels the effects of budget cutbacks. Right now the job market for volcanologists isn't very good, and full-time jobs are few and far between.

While you're in college you'll need to work with your advisor to select a graduate school with a program geared toward your specific interests. Although you might be able to get a job with just a four-year college degree, you'll be limited to working as an assistant or technician. If you really want to work as a volcanologist, you'll need a Ph.D. in geology, requiring another four or five years of school after college.

Once you get to graduate school, you'll start to study all about volcanoes. After a year or two of general class work, you'll get involved in volcano research. Eventually you'll pick one volcano or one feature of volcanic activity to study. By the time you earn your graduate degree, you'll be an expert on that topic.

Dr. Ken Hon, volcanologist

If you're going to spend your days studying volcanoes, you need to like being outside. For Ken Hon, that's no problem.

"When I got to college, I wanted to do something in the mountains," explains Hon, who grew up in Colorado. His first interest was ecology, but after climbing glaciers, he switched his major to geology. Fascinated with volcanoes during his undergraduate studies, he decided to focus on this aspect of geology in graduate school, while he also worked as a student researcher with the U.S. Geological Survey. Once he completed his Ph.D., he was offered a position at the Hawaiian Volcano Observatory (HVO) to spend three years studying lava flow.

"I like seeing things in nature that amaze me," Hon says. "You see the whole world in a different way. I'm constantly amazed. You can't imagine all the things a volcano can do!" Nowadays, Hon teaches geology at the University of Hawaii at Hilo (UHH), which gives him the chance to study the only active volcano in the United States while working with other volcanologists at the HVO. In his free time, Hon can often be found making educational films of volcanic eruptions with his wife, volcanologist Cheryl Gansecki, Ph.D.

Hon explains that working on an active volcano requires common sense and good intuition in judging whether a situation is safe. "Experience definitely plays a part in assessing a situation," he stresses.

To future volcanologists, he recommends taking as much math, physics, and chemistry as possible in high school and college. Hon also encourages students to explore the option of going to college in Hawaii. Not only does this offer the chance to study in a beautiful environment—it's the only place in the United States where you can go to college and have an active volcano in your backyard!

In fact, with Kilauea (one of the world's most active volcanoes), Mauna Loa (the earth's largest volcano), and HVO all within 30 miles of the University of Hawaii at Hilo, you'll have access to experiences and opportunities you can't get anyplace else. When it comes to costs, Hon notes that some good bargains make it possible to study in Hawaii for much less than you'd think. Students can earn an undergraduate degree at University of Hawaii at Hilo and then apply to graduate school at a branch campus in Manoa.

"Your mother won't be very happy with your choice [to become a volcanologist]," Hon jokes. "But pursue what you love, and don't be so tied to outcomes."

After graduate school, it will be time to look for a job. If you're lucky enough to find a full-time job as a volcanologist, you'll probably be working for the U.S. Geological Survey (USGS) at one of their five volcano observatories, or at the USGC Western Region Center in Menlo Park, California.

The oldest observatory is located on the rim of the Kilauea volcano located in Hawaii Volcanoes National Park on the Big Island of Hawaii. There is an observatory in Vancouver, Washington, where scientists monitor Mount Saint Helens and other Cascade volcanoes. More than 100 active Alaskan volcanoes are monitored by the Alaska Volcano Observatories with locations in Anchorage and Fairbanks. The Long Valley Caldera Observatory monitors the Long Valley Caldera from the USGS Western Regional Headquarters.

The newest observatory is at Yellowstone National Park, where volcanologists study and monitor the Yellowstone Plateau volcanic field.

You might also be able to find a job working for a state geologic survey, especially in states with active volcanoes, such as California, Oregon, and Washington. But chances are, with a Ph.D. in volcanology, at some point you'll work as a geology professor at a university. During your time off from teaching, summer and sabbaticals, you'll be able to do volcanic fieldwork—visiting volcanoes and studying more about them.

Pitfalls

There are very few full-time job opportunities for volcanologists. If you do find a job, you'll be working on an active volcano, which could erupt at any time without warning. And, chances are, you'll have to relocate.

Perks

Volcanologists have the opportunity to live in or travel to beautiful and often exotic locations studying an interesting natural phenomenon.

Get a Jump on the Job

To study geology and then volcanology, you need to take math and science classes in middle school or junior high and high school. Score well in algebra, trigonometry, pre-calculus, biology, chemistry, physics, and Earth science. You should also know how to use a computer and how to write simple computer programs. In college, try to go on as many geology field trips as you can, especially if you go to a college in an area where you'll have a chance to see volcanoes or volcanic rocks. You should also take advantage of internships and volunteer opportunities.

WHITE-WATER RAFTING GUIDE

OVERVIEW

You wake up in the morning, grab a pair of shorts and a T-shirt, and head out to the river at your local national park, where you lather on suntan lotion and throw a raft in the river for an exciting float under the summer sun through a scenic gorge. You've just arrived at work—if you're a white-water rafting expert.

If you think you'd like to jump into this career, there are plenty of swift-moving rivers you might work on. Some of the most famous river rapids in the country include the Snake River and Colorado River (through the Grand Canyon), but there are thousands of rivers in every state that offer white-water rafting trips. Since these channels are still being carved by erosion, you'll need to know how to navigate around numerous boulders and layers of hard bedrock in the river's path, creating vortices of swirling or funneled water, natural ramps, and sudden drops in elevation.

Rapids are generally classified on a scale of 1 to 5; class 1 rapids are just slightly more exciting than a calm river, while Class 5 rapids are likely to give you some serious thrills. While there are rivers in the United States considered Class 6, very few outfitters offer expeditions on them because of the extreme danger involved. (If you're determined to find adventure as a white-water rafting guide, the Blue Nile River in Africa has rapids that are classified from 1 to 10. Not only is this river far

more dangerous than any U.S. river, the Blue Nile has the added challenges of African crocodiles, sleeping death, malaria, and roaming bandits.)

Your duties as a white-water rafting guide might include loading rafts with equipment in the morning and making sure the raft is safely prepared for the trip. You'll greet guests, brief them on what to expect, and give them a safety speech. Other typical duties for raft guides often include working at the company's office, making reservations, renting equipment, and helping organize and sell retail goods. Employees also may help guests find

Schandra "Sunshine" Loveless, white-water rafting guide

There's never a boring day on the river," says Schandra Loveless, who guides rafters on Tennessee's class 3 Ocoee River. "It's always an adventure, although—because it's outdoor recreation—there are always dangers involved."

Loveless first became interested in being a white-water rafting guide after taking her first trip down the river. "I couldn't believe you could do this and get paid for it," she says. "It only takes one time!" She was required to be trained and certified in CPR and in basic first aid before becoming a guide. Older guides are also required to be certified in wilderness first aid. Each rafting company in Tennessee is responsible for their own training and the certifications they require.

Because the Ocoee is a dam-controlled river, they can raft between April and late October. "A lot of people make this job year round by going to other rivers," she explains. "Some go to ski resorts and then come back when it's time to run the river again."

Loveless rafts in all sorts of weather, rain or shine, hot or cold, "as long as the lightning isn't hitting right in front of the raft," she laughs. "It's fun because you meet all kinds of people. Even our bad days are better than the good days in an office."

lodging at nearby campgrounds, or set up a volleyball court where clients can play after the trip.

You'll need to be confident in the water and have good people skills. You also need to be able to communicate with people who don't understand English, are scared, or can't swim. You should be open-minded and patient, since customers often can't paddle and misunderstand instructions.

Having enthusiasm and being able to motivate your crew is essential. The most important part of the job is to make sure guests enjoy themselves, so you're often as much of an entertainer as a raft guide. Your job is to make the experience fun and keep the guests entertained. People who have a dynamic and playful personality make the best raft guides, because you need to keep everyone smiling and laughing the whole way.

You can learn how to be a rafting guide at one of the many schools advertised on the Internet. Basically, these schools teach river dynamics and hydrology, river-reading skills, properly rigging rafts for commercial or private trips, raft construction and maintenance, river and rafting terminology, rafting safety, the latest in river rescue skills and techniques, group leadership, ice-breakers and fun group games, food preparation, and health concerns in the outdoors. Many schools also provide internationally recognized certification as a swiftwater rescue technician.

Pitfalls

Low pay, few (if any) benefits, and job uncertainty are among the pitfalls of this position. In the western United States, the weather allows for rafting only from May to August; in the east the season extends from March to October. Once the rafting season ends, guides must find jobs for fall and winter. Rafting is also mentally and physically tiring, and often involves long bus rides each side of a river trip. If you don't think you can be enthusiastic in difficult situations, guiding isn't the right career for you.

Perks

If you love the outdoors and hate to be tied down to a desk—and you also love people—then white-water rafting can be an exhilarating career. You'll get to meet all sorts of interesting folks who have the same passions you do. You'll have plenty of free river trips and kayaking opportunities, and you'll have lots of freedom!

Get a Jump on the Job

If you think you might like to be a white-water rafting guide someday, get involved now in white-water sports (such as kayaking) so you get a feel for the water. Learn your knots—the more skills you have, the quicker you'll start earning money. Take up swimming, and something that develops your communication and public speaking skills. You'll also need to be prepared to volunteer your time to become an accredited guide and be ready to pay for your own training.

APPENDIX A. ASSOCIATIONS, ORGANIZATIONS, AND WEB SITES

ADVENTURE TRAVEL GUIDE

Adventure Travel Society
332 1/2 West Sackett Street
Salida, CO 81201
(719) 530-0171
ats@adventuretravel.com
http://www.adventuretravel.com

ATS is an international consulting firm dedicated to promoting natural resource sustainability, economic viability, and cultural integrity through sustainable tourism development.

Adventure Travel Trade Association
332 1/2 West Sackett Street
Salida, CO 81201
(719) 530-0171
ats@adventuretravel.biz
http://www.adventuretravel.biz

ATTA is an international trade association that helps members manage and market adventure travel and ecotourism, and facilitates communication and business relationships worldwide.

International Ecotourism Society
733 15th Street, NW, Suite 1000
Washington, DC 20005
(202) 347-9203
ecomail@ecotourism.org
http://www.ecotourism.org

Founded in 1990, TIES is the largest and oldest organization in the world dedicated to generating and disseminating information about ecotourism, with members in more than 70 countries. The organization's membership includes academics, consultants, conservation professionals and organizations, governments, architects, tour operators, lodge owners and managers, general development experts, and ecotourists. As a non-governmental organization, TIES is unique in its efforts to provide guidelines and standards, training, technical assistance, research and publications to foster sound ecotourism development join the growing ranks of ecotourism professionals who are working with the society to make tourism a viable tool for conservation, poverty alleviation, protection of culture and biodiversity, sustainable development, and educational travel.

Mountain Madness
4218 Southwest Alaska Street #206
Seattle, WA 98116
(800) 328-5925
http://www.mountainmadness.com

Adventure company dedicated to safely bringing the beauty and excitement of adventure to those who pursue it. All Mountain Madness guides are skilled professionals selected based on their technical proficiency, proven safety records, careful judgment, patient and supportive teaching styles, and great personalities. All guides have been Wilderness First Responder certified and are proficient in technical rescue and evacuation skills, and are dedicated to the world of alpinism. Many guides have made first ascents and successful summits on major peaks from the Cascades to *Mt. Everest, and have educational backgrounds in fields such as natural history and cultural anthropology.*

National Tour Association
546 East Main Street
Lexington, KY 40508
(800) 682-8886
questions@ntastaff.com
http://www.ntaonline.com

Association for travel professionals with an interest in the packaged travel sector of the industry. The association brings together those who package travel—group as well as individual trips—with suppliers and destinations representing the various components of a trip. Although based in North America, membership spans the globe.

ADVENTURE TRAVEL WRITER

American Society for Journalists and Authors
1501 Broadway, Suite 302
New York, NY 10036
(212) 997-0947
http://www.asja.org

Founded in 1948, the American Society of Journalists and Authors is the nation's leading organization of independent nonfiction writers.

Society of American Travel Writers
1500 Sunday Drive, Suite 102
Raleigh, NC 27607
(919) 861-5586
satw@satw.org
http://www.satw.org/satw/index.asp

Now in its 48th year, SATW is a nonprofit professional association whose purpose is to promote responsible journalism, provide professional support and development for members, and encourage the conservation

and preservation of travel resources worldwide.

AIR TRAFFIC CONTROLLER

Airline Dispatchers Federation
700 13th Street, Suite 950
Washington, DC 20005
(800) OPN-CNTL
http://www.dispatcher.org

The Airline Dispatchers Federation is the only national organization representing the professional interests of the dispatch profession, working for licensed aircraft dispatchers and operational control professionals from 103 aerospace companies including every major U.S. airline. It has been estimated that approximate 92% of airline passengers traveling each day in the United States do so under the watchful eye of ADF members.

Air Traffic Control Quarterly
Air Traffic Control Association INC
2300 Clarendon Boulevard, Suite 711
Arlington, VA 22201

A magazine for the air traffic control industry.

AviationNow: Careers
http://www.aviationnow.com/content/careercenter/global/car2001f.htm

A Web site with a selection of the latest news and analysis from the industry's leading publications, as well as complementary content created by AviationNow.com's team of editors. The careers section includes information about jobs, news on upcoming conferences and workshops, job listings, and bulletin boards.

FAA Air Traffic Control Division
http://www.ama500.jccbi.gov

A Web site discussing "how to become an air traffic controller."

Federal Aviation Administration (FAA)
800 Independence Avenue, SW
Washington, DC 20591
http://www.faa.gov
This primary Web site of the FAA, the governmental agency with the responsibility for providing a safe, secure, and efficient global aerospace system that contributes to national security and the promotion of U.S. aerospace safety. The FAA is the leading authority in the international aerospace community.

Flight Safety Digest
Flight Safety Foundation
601 Madison Street, Suite 300
Alexandria, VA 22314
(703) 739-6700
http://www.flightsafety.org
A magazine aimed at flight safety.

National Air Traffic Controllers Association
1325 Massachusetts Avenue, NW
Washington, DC 20005
(202) 223-2900
http://www.natca.org/about/career.msp
This Web page discusses: "So you want to be an air traffic controller?"

National Association of Air Traffic Specialists
11303 Amherst Avenue, Suite 4
Wheaton, MD 20902
(301) 933-6228
http://www.naats.org
This Web site offers lots of information for air traffic controllers.

ARCHEOLOGIST

A. Summer programs in archeology

Anasazi Heritage Center
Bureau of Land Management

27501 Highway 184
Dolores, CO 81323
(970) 882-4811
http://www.co.blm.gov/ahc/hmepge.htm
The Anasazi Heritage Center (AHC) is a museum of the Ancestral Puebloan (or Anasazi) culture and other Native cultures in the Four Corners region. It is also the starting point for visits to Canyons of the Ancients National Monument. AHC periodically offers student internships in collections management, exhibit/interpretive media, and museum education/ interpretation:

- Collections Management. *This internship involves a variety of curatorial tasks. The intern will be entering a considerable amount of data in the museum's ARGUS cataloging system. In addition, the intern will assist with various repackaging, reorganizing, and inventory projects of existing collections at the AHC. This position offers a broad exposure to the curatorial operations of a federal repository.*

- Exhibit and Interpretive Media. *Interns may work on improvements to the permanent exhibits in the main exhibits gallery, which are mainly based on materials available from AHC collections. The museum has a special interest in interactive and hands-on exhibit formats, and maintains a series of traveling exhibits for loan. Occasionally an internship is available to administer this program. Work may include loan tracking, marketing, repairs or enhancements to existing exhibits, and/or development of new exhibit offerings. The AHC hosts three to five temporary exhibitions annually in its special exhibit gallery, usually borrowed from other institutions, but they may be produced in-house or draw from a combination of resources. Interns sometimes contribute to the installation or enhancement of these exhibitions, depending on circumstances and need. One periodically available internship opportunity focuses on the Chappell Collection including nearly 1,000 ceramic vessels plus organic and ornamental objects representing the Pueblo II - Pueblo III period of Ancestral Puebloan occupation of this region. The Chappell intern develops and installs a thematic exhibit, working closely with the AHC Curator and Exhibit Specialist; however, development and installation of the exhibit will be primarily the intern's responsibility. The AHC is headquarters for Canyons of the Ancients National Monument, so other opportunities may involve creation of outdoor installations or interpretive literature for hikers and other non-museum recreational users.*

- Museum Education/ Interpretation. *Responsibilities include developing and presenting two educational and/or interpretive programs at the Anasazi Heritage Center (AHC). The programs focus on the prehistoric culture of the Ancestral Puebloans, the Four Corners area natural history (ecology, geology, etc.), Four Corners cultures, archeological scientific methods, and land management practices. Program formats may*

include hiking tours, short art demonstrations, impromptu lectures, one- to two-hour children's classes, or preparation of an educational tool such as an artifact loan box or an activity booklet. Additional responsibilities will include providing information and collecting entry fees at the front desk and operating the museum shop cash register.

Center for American Archaeology
Department B, Kampsville
Archaeological Center
PO Box 366
Kampsville, IL 62053
(618) 653-4316
http://www.caa-archeology.org

Originally formed in 1953, the CAA's mission is to discover and disseminate the unwritten story of earlier Americans' lifeways, accomplishments, and changing natural environment. Through integrated programs of archeological investigation, educational outreach, and cultural stewardship, the CAA strives to accomplish this mission.

For information on current internships and special programs, visit the CAA programs Web site at http:// caa-archeology.org/html/programs .htm#womenintern.

Crow Canyon Archaeological Center
Dept. AM
23390 County Road K
Cortez, CO 81321
(800) 422-8975
http://www.crowcanyon.org

The Crow Canyon Archaeological Center has conducted excavation and research at ancient Pueblo Indian sites in the American Southwest for almost two decades. In the Family Adventure Vacation at Crow Canyon, the program is designed with all generations in mind—parents, grandparents, and children who are 12 or older. The archeological educators find just the right balance of activities involving all family members, including evening programs on topics like rock art and traditional storytelling. The 170-acre campus provides plenty of space for relaxing, watching wildlife, walking through the pinyon and juniper woods, or enjoying panoramic mountain views from the rocking chairs on the lodge deck. Thousands of participants have, since 1983, been a part of Crow Canyon's research in the vast archeological region surrounding Mesa Verde National Park. Working alongside professional research archeologists, families contribute to important new insights into the ancestral Pueblo Indian (the Anasazi) communities that once flourished in this spectacular land of mesas, mountains, and canyons. Through participation in archeological excavation and laboratory analysis, you can make a real contribution to our research—and have fun doing it!

Earthwatch

Earthwatch Membership Service
Earthwatch Institute
3 Clock Tower Place
Suite 100
PO Box 75
Maynard, MA 01754-0075
(800) 776-0188
http://www.earthwatch.org/subject/archaeology.html

Earthwatch Institute engages people worldwide in scientific field research and education; students can participate on an Earthwatch archeological research expedition at sites from St. Croix to Madagascar. Earthwatch supports more than 140 expeditions in 48 countries, and sends 3,700 members of the public a year into the field to work side-by-side with leading scientists. Programs include:

- archaeology at West Point Foundry (teasing out technological, economic, and social history from the ruins of a 19th-century foundry)

- unearthing evidence of two radically different but contemporaneous societies from 3,000 years ago on the Chilean coast

- documenting the history and architecture of family lineage compounds to encourage their preservation at China's ancestral temples

- excavating shell middens to determine the impact of prehistoric humans on their environment in coastal Maine

- rescuing the heritage at the Olduvai Gorge

- exploring a rich Palaeolithic site for evidence of hominid adaptation to shifting environments in India

- excavating a particularly rich site in Andalusia to establish when and how humans first came to Europe

- uncovering the seeds of environmental degradation and cultural disintegration on Easter Island

- laying the groundwork for excavating an area that may prove to be a previously unknown independent kingdom in early England

- *documenting the historical and environmental conservation needs of harbor islands for listing as a World Heritage site in Mauritius*

- *investigating how culturally different populations develop alliances over time at a French fort in Virginia*

- *surveying an unexplored Maya site to reveal its role in regional cultural development*

Four Corners School of Outdoor Education
East Route
Monticello, UT 84535
(801) 587-2156
http://www.fourcornersschool.org

Four Corners School of Outdoor Education is a nonprofit organization founded in 1984, based in Monticello, Utah. Four Corners School specializes primarily in Arizona, Colorado, New Mexico, Utah, and Wyoming. The outdoor education programs have served some 25,000 participants ranging in age from 6 to 90, working to protect over 20 archeological sites on public lands. Field seminars are organized in cooperation with organizations such as the Denver Museum of Nature and Science, Sierra Club, Wilderness Society, National Geographic Society, Utah Museum of Natural History, and many others. Educational activities are conducted via rafting, backpacking, hiking, cultural experiences, and service work, and are led by experts in archaeology, geology, botany, biology, and/or Native American cultures. College credit is available through Fort Lewis College (Durango, Colo.), Prescott College, (Prescott, Ariz.), and the Colorado School of Mines (Golden, Colo.).

B. For more information about archeology as a career, contact the following organizations:

Archaeological Institute of America
Boston University
656 Beacon Street, 4th Floor
Boston, MA 02215-2006
(617) 353-9361
aia@bu.edu
http://www.archaeological.org

The AIA supports the aspirations of archeologists in a number of ways. The AIA provides research fellowships to allow young archeologists to increase their participation in excavations and to learn from the nation's leading archeologists. The AIA also publishes Archaeology magazine.

The AIA is North America's oldest and largest organization dedicated to archeological research, education, and conservation. The AIA also offers tours accompanied by one or more of the Institute's professional members— practicing archeologists who give you behind the scenes views of the sites on your tour. You will be privy to the sort of knowledge and firsthand insights that only an expert scholar can provide.

National Park Service, Archeological Division
Publication Coordinator
PO Box 37127
Washington, DC 20013-7127

The NPS publishes a brochure, Participate in Archeology, that lists books and videos on archaeology. For a copy, write to the above address.

Society for American Archaeology
900 Second Street, NE, Suite 12
Washington, DC 20002-3557
(202) 789-8200
headquarters@saa.org
http://www.saa.org

This group offers a brochure, Archaeology & You, available for $4; describes the training required to become a professional archeologist.

The Society for Historical Archaeology
PO Box 30446
Tucson, AZ 85751-0446
(520) 886-8006
sha@azstarnet.com
http://www.sha.org

This group provides information on training and job opportunities in the United States.

The Student Conservation Association
PO Box 550
Charlestown, NH 03603
(603) 543-1700
http://www.sca-inc.org

The Student Conservation Association (SCA) provides high school and college students alike with meaningful conservation service internships and volunteer opportunities in national parks, forests, and other public lands. Archeological internships include working at Canyon de Chelly National Monument, where students learn about and help catalog southwestern Indian history from the Archaic Period to the present while serving at the base of sheer red cliffs and canyon wall caves in Arizona. Students work closely with archeologists in the photographic archives, cataloging historic and modern photographs into a searchable database, and helping park archeologists with fieldwork.

Internships are also available at the Whiskeytown, Calif., national recreation area, where students will research the rich history of Whiskeytown. Historically the Whiskeytown area was the location of much mining activity dating back to the California Gold Rush. Students collect GPS location data and take field notes to document historic mining ditches, orchards, and resources, scan photographs and documents, catalog maps and slides, and compile project archives for completed projects, help researchers with records and research at local historical society and historical record sources, and assist archeologists with fieldwork, including field survey and site recording.

C. Archeology Web sites

About Archaeology
http://archaeology.about.com/science/archaeology

Ancient World Web
http://www.julen.net/ancient

Anthropology in the News: Archaeology News Archives
http://www.tamu.edu/news.html

Archaeology Magazine
http://www.archaeology.org

Archaeology on the Net
http://members.tripod.com/~archonnet

Archnet
http://archnet.uconn.edu

Careers in Archaeology FAQ
http://www.museum.state.il.us/ismdepts/anthro/dlcfaq.html

Current Archaeology
http://www.archaeology.co.uk

Discover Archaeology
http://www.discoveringarchaeology.com

European Archaeology Web Links
http://www.xs4all.nl/~mkosian/links.html

The Noise Room Archaeology News
http://www.thenoiseroom.com/frameset.
html

BLIMP PILOT

Fujifilm Blimp
Fuji Photo Film U.S.A., Inc. Corporate
Office
200 Summit Lake Drive, Floor 2
Valhalla, NY 10595
(914) 789-8100
http://www.fujifilm.com/JSP/fuji/
epartners/AboutBlimp.jsp

*This Web site features some information
about the specifications and crew of the the
Fujifilm blimp. You also can read some fun
facts about the ship and its travels.*

Goodyear Blimp
Goodyear Tire Corporate Headquarters
1144 East Market Street
Akron, OH 44316-0001
(330) 796-2121
http://www.goodyearblimp.com

*Each blimp has its own Web page. The
page includes the technical statistics
and specification of the ship along with
information about that particular blimp.*

- *The Spirit of America: http://www.
  goodyearblimp.com/fleet/spirit_
  america.html*
- *The Spirit of Goodyear: http://
  www.goodyearblimp.com/fleet/
  spirit_goodyear.html*
- *The Stars and Stripes: http://www.
  goodyearblimp.com/fleet/stars_
  stripes.html*

MetLife Blimp
Metropolitan Life Insurance Company
Corporate Home Office
200 Park Avenue

New York, NY 10166
http://www.metlife.com/Applications/
Corporate/WPS/CDA/PageGenerator/
0,1674,P309,00.html

*Information about the MetLife blimp
program and their ships "Snoopy One"
and "Snoopy Two."*

BOUNTY HUNTER

National Institute of Bail Enforcement
PMB 268 - 3105 North Ashland Avenue
Chicago, IL 60657
(815) 675-0260
http://www.bounty-hunter.net/contact.
htm

*A training facility offering skills
necessary to succeed in bounty hunting,
teaching the laws, language, tracking
skills, transportation, contracting,
handcuffing, foreign operations, fees,
and advertising knowledge necessary to
succeed in this trade.*

BULL RIDER

**Professional Rodeo Cowboys Association
(PRCA)**
101 ProRodeo Drive
Colorado Springs, CO 80919
(719) 593-8840
http://prorodeo.org

*The Professional Rodeo Cowboys
Association (PRCA) is the largest and
oldest rodeo organization in the world.
Almost 700 PRCA-sanctioned rodeos
are held each year, paying out over $34
million.*

Professional Bull Riders, Inc. (PBR)
6 South Tejon Street, Suite 700
Colorado Springs, CO 80903
(719) 471-3008
http://www.pbrnow.com

Unlike traditional rodeo associations, the Professional Bull Riders, Inc. (PBR) is dedicated to making bull riding a standalone sport. The PBR tour includes 29-cities and $10 million in prizes

RodeoAttitude.com
http://www.rodeoattitude.com

This huge site is dedicated to all things rodeo, including information about associations, events, breeders, arenas, and other rodeo sources. You'll also find links to more information about each individual rodeo event (including bull riding) and links to the homepages of many rodeo personnel and athletes. You can even connect with other rodeo fans and professionals through message boards and forums.

Women's Professional Rodeo Association
1235 Lake Plaza Drive Suite 127
Colorado Springs, CO 80906
(719) 576-0900
http://www.wpra.com

While many people think of bull riding and other rodeo events as a "guy-thing," many women can and do compete in rodeo events, including bull riding.

CHIMNEY SWEEP

Chimney Safety Institute of America
2155 Commercial Drive
Plainfield, IN 46168
(317) 837-5362
office@csia.org
http://www.csia.org

A nonprofit educational organization dedicated to chimney and venting system safety and committed to the elimination of residential chimney fires, carbon monoxide intrusion, and

other chimney-related hazards that result in the loss of lives and property. To achieve these goals, CSIA devotes its resources to educating the public, chimney and venting professionals, and other fire prevention specialists about the prevention and correction of chimney and venting system hazards.

National Chimney Sweep Guild
2155 Commercial Drive
Plainfield, IN 46168
(317) 837-1500
http://www.ncsg.org

The guild provides progressive services, encouraging professionalism and ethical accountability, and advancing the chimney and venting industry through public awareness of the trade.

National Chimney Sweep Training School
Chimney Safety Institute of America
Technology Center
2155 Commercial Drive
Plainfield, IN 46168
(317) 837-5362
office@csia.org
http://www.csia.org/professionals/ncsts
.htm

The National Chimney Sweep Training School provides an educational opportunity for anyone interested in the chimney service field for newcomers and an excellent review of standard practices for anyone already working in the field. The in-depth, six-day course teaches the basic skills chimney professionals use every day. Sponsored by the Chimney Safety Institute of America, the course gives students the opportunity to learn about the most up-to-date tools, technologies, and standards.

COAST GUARD OFFICER

U.S. Coast Guard
http://www.gocoastguard.com
Web site provides information about the Coast Guard, including how to find a recruiter, scholarships, and information about training and jobs.

U.S. Coast Guard Academy
31 Mohegan Avenue
New London, CT 06320-8103
(800) 883-USCG (8724)
http://www.cga.edu
The United States Coast Guard Academy was founded in 1876 and is one of the most selective colleges in America. The smallest of the five federal service academies, the Coast Guard Academy provides a four-year bachelor of science program with a full scholarship for each individual. Unlike other federal service academies, there are no congressional appointments.

U.S. Coast Guard Auxiliary
http://www.cgaux.org
The U.S. Coast Guard Auxiliary was established by Congress in 1939 to help the Coast Guard promote boating safety. It includes more than 35,000 members from all walks of life who receive special training so that they may be a functional part of Coast Guard Forces. Auxiliarists assist the Coast Guard in non–law enforcement programs such as public education, vessel safety checks, safety patrols, search and rescue, maritime security and environmental protection, and Coast Guard Academy introduction programs for youth.

U.S. Coast Guard Recruiters
(877) NOW-USCG
http://www.gocoastguard.com/offices/recindex.htm

U.S. Coast Guard Reserve
http://www.uscg.mil/hq/reserve/reshmpg.html
The U.S. Coast Guard Reserve is the military reserve component of the U.S. Coast Guard, one of the five armed forces of the United States. The Coast Guard Reserve provides trained and qualified personnel available for active duty in time of war or national emergency. The Coast Guard's mix of military, civil law enforcement, and regulatory authorities allow it to respond to a wide variety of national security missions at home and abroad, including deployed harbor defense/port security (HD/PS), Homeland Security, and Maritime Interdiction Operations (MIO).

COMMERCIAL DIVER

Association of Commercial Diver Educators (ACDE)
http://www.diveweb.com/acde/members.html
This Web site provides a list of accredited diver education schools.

Association of Diving Contractors International
5206 FM 1960 West, Suite 202
Houston, TX 77069
(281) 893-8388
http://www.adc-usa.org
The goal of the Association of Diving Contractors International, Inc. (ADCI) is to promote commercial diving, establish safety standards, and encourage all dive companies to observe those standards. The ADCI has more than 400 member companies.

Underwater Magazine
http://www.diveweb.com/uw

This bi-monthly journal of the ADCI maintains an online archive at http://www.diveweb.com/uw/archives.

COOK IN ANTARTICA

Raytheon Polar Services
61 Inverness Drive East, Suite 300
Englewood, CO 80112
(303) 790-8606
resume@polar.org
http://www.polar.org/apc/employ/apply
.asp

If you're interested in working "on the ice," you should seriously consider attending one of Raytheon's Antarctica job fairs. While you won't have an in-depth interview, the face-to-face contact will probably be helpful given all the competition. Applicants can find application forms at Raytheon's Web site; you can send completed applications to the above address.

CORONER

International Association of Coroners and Medical Examiners
P.O. Box 44834
Columbus, OH 43204-0834
(614) 276-8384

This organization of elected lay and physician coroners also includes a small number of physician medical examiners.

International Homicide Investigators Association (IHIA)
http://www.ihia.org

This organization is the largest and fastest growing organization of homicide and death investigation professionals in the world and has representation from the United States and 16 other nations.

The National Association of Medical Examiners (NAME)
430 Pryor Street SW
Atlanta, GA 30312
(404) 730-4781
http://www.thename.org

This organization includes mainly physician medical examiners and other members of their death investigation teams. Physician pathologists and some physician coroners are also members. The NAME Web site includes a page entitled "So You Want To Be A Medical Detective?" that explains the differences between a coroner and a medical examiner and other experts who work on a death investigation: http://www.thename.org/medical_detective.htm

Statewide investigator information
http://www.cdc.gov/epo/dphsi/mecisp/
death_investigation.htm

Provides information about the requirements for death investigators in each state.

CRIME SCENE CLEANUP TECHNICIAN

American Bio-Recovery Association*
PO Box 828
Ipswich, MA 01938
(888) 979-2272
http://www.americanbiorecovery.org

This is a national nonprofit organization of crime and trauma scene recovery professionals.

* Note: If you decide to research this field for additional information, you might come across "before and after" photos, so that companies can show the quality of their work. Be warned that the "before" photos are often very graphic in nature and may be disturbing.

CYBERSLEUTH

American Society for Industrial Security (ASIS)
1625 Prince Street
Alexandria, VA 22314
(703) 519-6200
http://www.asisonline.org

ASIS International, with more than 33,000 members, is an international organization for professionals responsible for security, including managers and directors of security. In addition, corporate executives and other management personnel, as well as consultants, architects, attorneys, and federal, state, and local law enforcement, are becoming involved with ASIS to better understand the constant changes in security issues and solutions.

Cipher
http://www.ieee-security.org/cipher.html

Electronic newsletter of the technical committee on security and privacy, a technical committee of the computer society of the IEEE.

ComputerWorld
http://www.computerworld.com

Professional periodical for computer security.

High Technology Crimes Investigation Association
1474 Freeman Drive
Amissville, VA 20106
(540) 937-5019
http://htcia.org

Nonprofit group designed to encourage the exchange of data, information, experience, ideas, and knowledge about techniques related to investigations and security in advanced technologies.

Information Systems Security Association
7044 South 13th Street
Oak Creek, WI 53154
(414) 768-8000
http://www.issa.org

The Information Systems Security Association (ISSA) is a nonprofit, international organization of information security professionals and practitioners. It provides educational forums, publications, and peer interaction opportunities that enhance the knowledge, skill, and professional growth of its members. With active participation from individuals and chapters all over the world, the ISSA is the largest international, nonprofit association specifically for security professionals. Members include practitioners at all levels of the security field in a broad range of industries, such as communications, education, healthcare, manufacturing, finance, and government.

International Association of Computer Investigative Specialists (IACIS)
PO Box 21688
Kaizer, OR 97307
(503) 557-1506
http://www.cops.org

IACIS is an international volunteer nonprofit corporation composed of law enforcement professionals dedicated to education in the field of forensic computer science. IACIS members represent federal, state, local and international law enforcement professionals. Regular IACIS members have been trained in the forensic science of seizing and processing computer systems. IACIS is dedicated to the education and certification of law enforcement professionals in the field of computer forensic science, establishing procedures, training personnel, and certifying forensic examiners in the recovery of evidence from computer systems.

DRUG ENFORCEMENT ADMINISTRATION SPECIAL AGENT

Drug Enforcement Administration
Special Agent Recruitment
700 Army Navy Drive
Arlington, VA 22202
(800) DEA-4288
http://www.dea.gov

To find the recruitment coordinator nearest you, go to http://www.dea.gov/job/agent/recruiters.html.

ELECTRIC COMPANY LINEMAN

Communications Workers of America (CWA)
501 3rd Street, NW
Washington, DC 20001
(202) 434-1100
cwaweb@cwa-union.org
http://www.cwa-union.org

This organization can provide general information and some educational resources on line installer and repairer jobs.

International Brotherhood of Electrical Workers (IBEW)
Telecommunications Department
1125 15th Street, NW
Washington, DC 20005
(202) 833-7000
http://www.ibew.org

This organization can provide general information and some educational resources on line installer and repairer jobs.

EMERGENCY MEDICAL TECHNICIAN

National Association of Emergency Medical Technicians (NAEMT)
PO Box 1400
Clinton, MS 39060
http://www.naemt.org

The National Association of Emergency Medical Technicians represents the views of pre-hospital care personnel and influences the future advancement of EMS as an allied health profession. NAEMT offers educational programs, liaison activities, development of national standards and reciprocity, and development of programs to benefit pre-hospital care personnel.

National Registry of Emergency Medical Technicians (NREMT)
Rocco V. Morando Building
6610 Busch Boulevard
PO Box 29233
Columbus, OH 43229
http://www.nremt.org

National Highway Transportation Safety Administration, EMS Division
400 7th Street, SW, NTS-14
Washington, DC 20590
http://www.nhtsa.dot.gov/portal/site/nhtsa/menuitem.2a0771e91315babbbf30811060008a0c

FBI SPECIAL AGENT

Federal Bureau of Investigation
J. Edgar Hoover Building
935 Pennsylvania Avenue, NW
Washington, D.C. 20535-0001
(202) 324-3000
http://www.fbi.gov

FBI Agents Association
http://www.fbiaa.org/home.htm

FBI Famous Cases
http://www.fbi.gov/libref/historic/
famcases/famcases.htm

FEDERAL AIR MARSHAL

Federal Aviation Administration (FAA)
http://www.faa.gov/

The FAA Web site provides more information on Civil Aviation Security Specialist (CASS) positions (which include federal air marshals).

FAA Career Opportunities Page
http://jobs.faa.gov

This Web site has links to application forms and additional information.

FISHING GUIDE

Professional Guides Association of America
2416 South Eads Street
Arlington, VA 22202-2532
(703) 892-5757

GRAND CANYON HELICOPTER PILOT

Helicopter Association International
1635 Prince Street
Alexandria, VA 22314
(703) 683-4646
http://www.rotor.com

This nonprofit professional association is dedicated to promoting the helicopter as a safe and efficient method of transportation.

HELICOPTER TRAFFIC REPORTER

National Broadcast Pilots Association (NBPA)
http://www.nbpa.rotor.com

This organization is designed for pilots and crew members flying ENG helicopters and aircrafts for both television and radio. To learn more about the ENG equipment the pilots/reporters use, check out the following companies: EAC Helicopters Inc.(http://www.eachelicopters.com); Helicopters, Inc. (http://www. heliinc.com); Sky Helicopters, Inc. (http://www.skyhelicopters.com); U.S. Helicopters, Inc. (http://www. ushelicoptersinc.com).

Helicopter Association International
1635 Prince Street
Alexandria, VA 22314
(703) 683-4646
http://www.rotor.com

This nonprofit professional association is dedicated to promoting the helicopter as a safe and efficient method of transportation.

HIGH-RISE WINDOW WASHER

American Window Cleaner
http://www.awcmag.com

This professional window cleaners' magazine covers all aspects of the window washing trade. The Web site includes more information about the magazine, including how to subscribe.

International Window Cleaning Association (IWCA)
6418 Grovedale Drive, #101B
Alexandria, VA 22310-2571
(800) 875-4922
http://www.iwca.org

This nonprofit trade association is committed to raising the standards of professionalism and safety within the window cleaning industry.

International Window Cleaner
Certification Institute (IWCCI)
IWCCI Headquarters
6418 Grovedale Drive, #101B
Alexandria, VA 22310-2571
(703) 971-7771
info@iwcci.org
http://www.iwcci.org

This nonprofit organization offers a window cleaner certification program.

HOT-AIR BALLOON PILOT

Balloon Federation of America (BFA)
PO Box 400
Indianolo, IA 50125
(515) 961-8809
http://www.bfa.net

This nonprofit volunteer organization represents the interests of more than 3,500 hot-air balloon pilots and their crews. Anyone with an interest in ballooning can join. The BFA holds educational and safety training programs, and organizes and runs competitions (including the U.S. National Balloon Championships). The BFA also publishes Ballooning, a bimonthly magazine on ballooning and balloonists, and they sponsor the BFA Junior Balloonist program.

Balloon Life
http://www.balloonlife.com.

This magazine is dedicated to hot-air ballooning. The Web site includes more information, including how to subscribe.

BFA Junior Balloonist program
http://bfa.net/jrballoonists/index.htm

eHotAirBallooning
http://ehotairballooning.com

This Web site is a great place to find all sorts of information about hot air

ballooning—everything from discussions to organizations, competition, events, and clubs.

HURRICANE HUNTER

53rd Weather Reconnaissance Squadron
(Hurricane Hunters)
http://www.hurricanehunters.com

This Web site offers pictures, movie clips, answers to frequently asked questions, a virtual cyber flight, and more. To learn more about individual crew duties, visit: http://www.hurricanehunters.com/ faccrew.htm.

Each of the positions on the hurricane hunters' team has different educational, eligibility, and additional qualifications. You need to select your specialty early on so that you can meet those requirements.

- *Details about pilot jobs: http://www .hurricanehunters.com/jobpi.htm.*

- *Details about navigator jobs: http:// www.hurricanehunters.com/jobnav. htm*

- *Details about aerial recon weather officer (ARWO) jobs: http://www. hurricanehunters.com/jobarwo.htm*

- *Details about flight engineer jobs: http://www.hurricanehunters.com/ jobeng.htm*

- *Details about dropsonde operator jobs: http://www.hurricanehunters. com/jobdso.htm*

U.S. Air Force Reserve
http://www.afreserve.com/home4.asp

To request additional information on becoming a member of the Air Force Reserve visit the Web site at http://www .afreserve.com/contact.asp or call (800) 257-1212 to speak with a recruiter.

LOBSTERMAN

The Lobster Conservancy
P.O. Box 235
Friendship, ME 04547
(207) 832-8224
http://www.lobsters.org/misc/contact.
html
Nonprofit group that tries to sustain a thriving lobster fishery through science and community.

LOGGER

When searching for additional information online, use the search word *logger* and not *lumberjack*. Most of the information found when you search using *lumberjack* is related to iron man/lumberjack competitions, not a career in logging.

American Loggers Council (ALC)
PO Box 2109
Cleveland, TX 77328
(281) 432-7167
http://www.americanloggers.org
The ALC is "The National Voice for Professional Loggers." Their Web site offers logging articles and information, and features an "Ask a Logger" area.

Forest Resources Association, Inc. (FRA)
http://www.forestresources.org
This Web site offers information about the forest products industry (which includes logging), together with links to other sites.

Logging and Sawmilling Journal and Timber West
http://www.forestnet.com

State logging information
http://www.forestresources.org/ALLIES/
state-assoc.html

Most states have a forestry, logging, or forest industry association; visit the above Web site to find out more information in your state.

TimberLine Magazine
http://www.timberlinemag.com/index.asp

Timber Harvesting Magazine
http://www.timberharvesting.com

MERCHANT MARINER

Maritime Administration (MARAD)
http://www.marad.dot.gov/acareerafloat/
index.htm
The U.M. Merchant Marine is regulated by the Department of Transportation's Maritime Administration (MARAD). The MARAD offers information on job training, job location, job descriptions, and much more. For information on merchant marine licensing and documentation: http://www.uscg.mil/ stcw/index.htm.

Seafarers International Union (SIU)
5201 Auth Way
Camp Springs, MD 20746
(301) 899-0675
http://www.seafarers.org
The Seafarers International Union (SIU) represents unlicensed U.S. merchant mariners sailing aboard U.S. flag vessels in the Atlantic, Gulf, Great Lakes, and inland waters. The SIU also operates the Paul Hall Center for Maritime Training Education in Piney Point, Maryland, which offers the most U.S. Coast Guard-approved courses of any maritime school in the nation.

U.S. Merchant Marine Academy
300 Steamboat Road
Kings Point, NY 11024

(866) 546- 4778
http://www.usmma.edu

MOUNTAIN GUIDE

Association for Experiential Education (AEE)
3775 Iris Avenue, Suite #4
Boulder, CO 80301-2043
(866) 522-8337
http://www.aee.org

The association is committed to support professional development, theoretical advancement, and evaluation of experiential education worldwide.

American Mountain Guides Association (AMGA)
PO Box 1739
Boulder, CO 80306
http://www.amga.com

A nonprofit organization that represents the interest of American mountain guides by providing support, education, and standards. The AMGA offers training courses and certification exams in three different disciplines: rock, alpine and ski mountaineering.

International Federation of Mountain Guide Associations (IFMGA)
http://www.ivbv.info/en/index.asp

NAVY SEAL

Great Lakes Naval Station
http://www.nsgreatlakes.navy.mil

Navy SEALs
http://www.navy.com/seals

Sea Cadets
http://www.seacadets.org/join

U.S. Navy
http://www.navy.com
To request more information, visit http://www.navy.com/moreinfo. To find a

recruiter in your area, visit: http://www.navy.com/recruiter.

OUTWARD BOUND LEADER

Association for Experiential Education (AEE)
3775 Iris Avenue, Suite #4
Boulder, CO 80301-2043
(866) 522-8337
http://www.aee.org

The association is committed to support professional development, theoretical advancement, and evaluation of experiential education worldwide.

Outward Bound
(845) 424-4000
http://www.outwardbound.com/contact.html

This organization conducts safe adventure-based programs structured to inspire self-esteem, self-reliance, concern for others, and care for the environment.

PRIVATE INVESTIGATOR

Academy of Legal Investigators (ALI)
3303 Ward Court NE
Salem, OR 97305
(800) 842-7421
http://www.investigatoracademy.com

Detective Training Institute (DTI)
PO Box 909
San Juan Capiustrano, CA 92693
(888) 425-9388
http://www.detectivetraining.com

International Association of Financial Crimes Investigators (IAFCI)
1620 Grant Avenue
Novato, CA 94945
(415) 897-8800
http://www.iafci.org

International Association of Special
Investigation Units (IASIU)
5024-R Campbell Boulevard
Baltimore, MD 21236
(410) 933-3480
http://www.iasiu.com

Lion Investigation Academy
Admissions Office
553 Main Street
Stroudsburg, PA 18360
(717) 223-5627
http://www.lioninvestigationacademy.
com

National Association of Investigative
Specialists (NAIS)
PO Box 33244
Austin, TX 78764
(512) 719-3595
http://www.pimall.com/nais/home.html
Web site offers PI daily Newspaper,
*forums, and links to other sites of
interest.*

National Association of Legal
Investigators (NALI)
6109 Meadowwood
Grand Blanc, MI 48439
(800) 266-6254
http://www.nali.com

PI Magazine
755 Bronx
Toledo, OH 43609
(419) 382-0967
http://www.pimagazine.com
PI Magazine *is the bimonthly journal of
professional investigators; its Web site
includes a list of upcoming conferences
and links to many related sites.*

Private investigator licensing
http://www.crimetime.com/licensing.htm
*This Web site offers licensing
requirements for your state.*

State private investigator associations
http://www.pimagazine.com/links_State_
Reg.htm
*Many states and regions have associations
for private investigators. To find one in
your area, check this Web site.*

PYROTECHNICIAN

American Fireworks News
http://www.fireworksnews.com
Newspaper for pyrotechnics.

American Pyrotechnics Association
(APA)
PO Box 30438
Bethesda, MD 20824
http://www.americanpyro.com

*The APA is the premier trade association
of the fireworks industry, founded in
1948 to encourage safety in the design
and use of all types of fireworks, to
provide industry information and
support, and to promote responsible
regulation of the fireworks industry.
Members include manufacturers,
displayers, wholesalers, retailers,
importers, and suppliers.*

Bureau of Alcohol, Tobacco, Firearms
and Explosives
Office of Liaison and Public Information
650 Massachusetts Avenue, NW
Room 8290
Washington, DC 20226
http://www.atf.treas.gov
*Government bureau responsible for
regulating fireworks.*

Office of Hazardous Materials Safety
400 7th Street, SW
Washington DC 20509
http://hazmat.dot.gov
*Government organization responsible for
fireworks.*

National Fireworks Association (NFA)
8224 NW Bradford Court
Kansas City, MO 64151
http://www.nationalfireworks.org

The National Fireworks Association dedicated to the safe use of fireworks. Formed in 1992, the NFA's goal is to protect the rights of individuals and companies to enjoy fireworks. Safety is a key concern.

National Council on Fireworks Safety
4808 Moorland Lane Suite 109
Bethesda, MD 20814
http://www.fireworksafety.com

Nonprofit organization dedicated to educating the public on pyrotechnics and safety.

Pyrotechnicians.com
http://pyrotechnicians.com

A Web site dedicated to pyrotechnicians' job board.

Pyrotechnics Guild International (PGI)
http://www.pgi.org

An independent worldwide nonprofit organization of amateur and professional fireworks enthusiasts. Its educational and scientific purposes are to promote the safe and responsible display and use of pyrotechnics and fireworks, and to channel the creative energies of talented people into the design, production, and display of high quality fireworks by example of the membership and through the sharing of knowledge.

RODEO CLOWN

Professional Rodeo Cowboys Association
101 ProRodeo Drive
Colorado Springs, CO 80919
(719) 593-8840
http://prorodeo.org

This association is the largest and oldest rodeo organization in the world.

RodeoAttitude.com
http://www.rodeoattitude.com

This Web site is dedicated to all things rodeo, with information about associations and events, and message boards for other rodeo fans and professionals.

Women's Professional Rodeo Association
1235 Lake Plaza Drive Suite 127
Colorado Springs, CO 80906
(719) 576-0900
http://www.wpra.com

While rodeo events are usually thought of as a "guy thing," women can and do work at rodeos as barrelmen and rodeo clowns. This association has information on all these jobs.

SECRET SERVICE AGENT

U.S. Secret Service
Personnel Division
245 Murray Drive, Building 410
Washington, DC 20223
(202) 406-5800
http://www.ustreas.gov/usss/faq.
shtml#protect

The United States Secret Service is mandated by statute and executive order to carry out two significant missions: protection and criminal investigations.

U.S. Secret Service Agency Web site: Job fair listings
http://www.ustreas.gov/usss/
opportunities_fairs.shtml

The U.S. Secret Service strongly encourages candidates to attend job fair events to learn more about career opportunities. With questions, you can contact the Secret Service office nearest you or contact the Recruiting & Hiring Coordinating Center at (202) 406-5830 for more information.

SKI PATROLLER

National Ski Patrol (NSP)
133 South Van Gordon Street, Suite 100
Lakewood, CO 80228
(303) 988-1111
http://www.nsp.org
Organization dedicated to education and safety for ski patrol workers.

Professional Ski Patrol Association
http://www.pspa.org
Organization dedicated to promoting the highest standards of ski patrolling. The Professional Ski Patrol Association educates, tests, and certifies patrollers in ski safety, first-aid skills, toboggan handling and ski techniques.

Ski Patrol Magazine
http://www.nsp.org/nsp2002/spm_
template.asp

SMOKEJUMPER

U.S. Bureau of Land Management (BLM)
http://www.fire.blm.gov
This Web site is dedicated to fire management services, with information about smokejumping and wildland fires.

U.S. Forest Service (FS)
http://www.fs.fed.us/fire
This Web site is dedicated to fire management services, with information about smokejumping and wildland fires.

International Association of Firefighters (IAFF)

1750 New York Avenue, NW
Washington, DC 20006
(202) 737-8484
http://www.iaff.com
National union for firefighters.

National Fire Protection Association (NFPA)
1 Batterymarch Park
Quincy, MA 02269
(617) 770-3000
http://www.nfpa.org
The mission of the international nonprofit NFPA is to reduce the worldwide burden of fire and other hazards on the quality of life by providing and advocating scientifically based consensus codes and standards, research, training, and education.

National Interagency Fire Center (NIFC)
3833 South Development Avenue
Boise, ID 83705-5354
(208) 387-5512
http://www.nifc.gov

National Smokejumper Association (NSA)
http://www.smokejumpers.com
This Web site has information for anyone interested in becoming a smokejumper, plus a forum dedicated to smokejumping. For an additional fee, you can get a subscription to Smokejumper Magazine.

Smokejumper bases
http://www.fs.fed.us/fire/people/
smokejumpers/bases.html
Each U.S. smokejumper base (except for the Grangeville [Idaho] Smokejumpers) has a Web site. The sites give additional information specific to that base, what they do at that base, additional details about qualifications and requirements for hiring, and lots of other important information.

- Alaska Smokejumpers—http://alaskasmokejumpers.com
- **Boise (Great Basin) Smokejumpers**—http://www.fire.blm.gov/smokejumper
- **McCall Smokejumpers**—http://www.fs.fed.us/fire/people/smokejumpers/mccall; http://www.mccallsmokejumpers.org (unofficial site)
- **Missoula Smokejumpers**—http://www.fs.fed.us/fire/people/smokejumpers/missoula
- **North Cascades Smokejumpers**—http://www.fs.fed.us/r6/oka/fire/ncsb
- **Redmond Smokejumpers**—http://www.fs.fed.us/fire/people/smokejumpers/RAC
- **Region 5 (Northern California) Smokejumpers**—http://www.fs.fed.us/fire/people/smokejumpers/redding
- **West Yellowstone Smokejumpers**—http://www.fs.fed.us/r1/gallatin/fire/wyifc/main.htm

Wildland Fire

http://www.wildlandfire.com

A Web site dedicated to wildland fire fighting.

Wildfire News

http://www.wildfirenews.com

A Web site dedicated to wildland fire fighting.

STEEPLEJACK

Steeplejack Industrial Group
http://www.steeplejack.ca/index2.htm

Steeplejacks of America
http://www.steepljk.com

TEXAS RANGER

Texas Ranger Association Foundation
104 Texas Ranger Trail
Waco, TX 76706
(254) 752-1001
TRAF_@email.msn.com
http://www.thetexasrangers.org

The Texas Ranger Association Foundation is a nonprofit group organized in 1982 to support the active and retired Texas Rangers of the Texas Department of Public Safety.

Texas Ranger Hall of Fame
Junior Texas Ranger Program
PO Box 2570
Waco, TX 76702-2570
(877) 750-8631
http://www.texasranger.org/jrRangers/jrRangers.htm

Today younger students can become Junior Texas Rangers through a special program of the Texas Ranger Hall of Fame and Museum. This nonprofit program supports the renovation and improvement of the museum and its educational programs. The first project is a new educational headquarters building, housing Texas Ranger Company "F" that children will be able to visit. Benefits of joining the Junior Rangers include:

- *honorary Junior Ranger appointment suitable for framing from the Texas Ranger Hall of Fame, signed by a real active duty Texas Ranger*
- *two Junior Ranger toy badges*
- *the Junior Ranger's name recorded on the museum internet site and at the Texas Ranger Hall of Fame and Museum*

Texas Ranger Hall of Fame & Museum
PO Box 2570
Waco, TX 76702-2570
(254)750-8631
http://www.texasranger.org
Museum filled with information and history about the Texas Rangers.

VOLCANOLOGIST

U.S. Geological Service
http://vulcan.wr.usgs.gov/Outreach/StudyVolcanoes
This Web site offers a page of links with information for future volcanologists.

Volcano Observatories
Each of the five observatories has its own Web page with pictures, information about what they do and the volcanoes they are monitoring, and much more.

- **Alaska Volcano Observatory (AVO)**—http://www.avo.alaska.edu
- **Cascades Volcano Observatory (CVO)**—http://vulcan.wr.usgs.gov/CVO_Info
- **Hawaiian Volcano Observatory (HVO)**—http://hvo.wr.usgs.gov
- **Long Valley Observatory (LVO)**—http://lvo.wr.usgs.gov/index.html
- **Yellowstone Volcano Observatory (YVO)**—http://volcanoes.usgs.gov/yvo

Volcano World
http://volcano.und.nodak.edu/vw.html
This Web site offers lots of volcano information; while you're there, check out the top 101 Ask a Volcanologist questions at http://volcano.und.nodak.edu/vwdocs/frequent_questions/top_101/Top_101.html.

WHITE-WATER RAFTING GUIDE

American Whitewater (AW)
1424 Fenwick Lane
Silver Spring, MD 20910
(866) BOAT-4-AW
http://www.americanwhitewater.org

The mission of American Whitewater is to conserve and restore America's white-water resources and to enhance opportunities to enjoy them safely. The association focuses on education through publication of its magazine, American Whitewater, and by providing education about white-water rivers, boating safety, technique, and equipment. AW maintains a complete national inventory of white-water rivers, monitors threats to those rivers, publishes information on river conservation, provides technical advice to local groups, works with government agencies, and—when necessary—takes legal action to prevent river abuse. The group also organizes sporting events, contests, and festivals to raise funds for river conservation, including the Ocoee Whitewater Rodeo in Tennessee and the annual Gauley River Festival in West Virginia, the largest gathering of white-water boaters in the nation. AW promotes paddling safety, publishes reports on white-water accidents, and maintains both a uniform national ranking system for white-water rivers (the International Scale of Whitewater Difficulty) as well as an internationally recognized white-water safety code.

APPENDIX B. ONLINE CAREER RESOURCES

This volume offers a look inside a wide range of unusual and unique careers that might appeal to someone with an adventurous spirit or personality. And while it highlights general information, it's really only a glimpse into the job. The entries are intended to merely whet your appetite, and provide you with some career options you may never have known existed.

Before jumping into any career, you'll want to do more research to make sure that it's really something you want to pursue. You'll most likely want to learn as much as you can about the careers in which you are interested. That way, as you continue to research and talk to people in those particular fields, you can ask informed and intelligent questions that will help you make your decisions. You might want to research the education options for learning the skills you'll need to be successful, along with scholarships, work-study programs, and other opportunities to help you finance that education. And, you might want answers to questions that were not addressed in the information provided here.

If you search long enough, you can find just about anything using the Internet, including additional information about the jobs featured in this book.

✳ **A word about Internet safety:** The Internet is a wonderful resource for networking. Many job and career sites have forums where students can interact with other people interested in and working in that field. Some sites even offer online chats where people can communicate with each other in real-time. They provide students and jobseekers opportunities to make connections and maybe even begin to lay the groundwork for future employment. But as you use these forums and chats, remember that anyone could be on the other side of that computer screen, telling you exactly what you want to hear. It's easy to get wrapped up in the excitement of the moment when you are on a forum or in a chat, interacting with people that share your career interests and aspirations. Be cautious about what kind of personal information you make available on the forums and in the chats; never give out your full name, address, or phone number. And never agree to meet with someone that you have met online.

SEARCH ENGINES

When looking for information, there are many search engines you could use besides the well-known Google to help you find out more about adventurous jobs. You may already have a favorite search engine, but you might want to take some time to check out some of the others. Some have features that might help you find information you couldn't locate anywhere else. Several engines offer suggestions for ways to narrow your results, or suggest related phrases you might want to use. This is handy if you are having trouble locating exactly what you want.

It's also a good idea to learn how to use the advanced search features of your favorite search engines. Knowing the advanced possibilities might help you to zero-in on exactly the information for which you're searching without wasting time looking through pages of irrelevant hits.

As you use the Internet to search information on the perfect career, keep in mind that like anything you find on the Internet, you need to consider the source from which the information comes.

Some of the most popular Internet search engines are:

AllSearchEngines.com
http://www.allsearchengines.com

This search engine index has links to the major search engines along with search engines grouped by topic. The site includes a page with more than 75 career and job search engines at http://www. allsearchengines.com/careerjobs.html.

AlltheWeb
http://www.alltheweb.com

AltaVista
http://www.altavista.com

Ask Jeeves
http://www.ask.com

Dogpile
http://www.dogpile.com

Excite
http://www.excite.com

Google
http://www.google.com

HotBot
http://www.hotbot.com

LookSmart
http://www.looksmart.com

Lycos
http://www.lycos.com

Mamma.com
http://www.mamma.com

MSN Network
http://www.msn.com

My Way
http://www.goto.com

Teoma
http://www.directhit.com

Vivisimo
http://www.vivisimo.com

Yahoo!
http://www.yahoo.com

HELPFUL WEB SITES

The Internet has a wealth of information on careers—everything from the mundane to the outrageous. There are thousands, if not millions, of sites devoted to helping you find the perfect job for you and your interests, skills, and talents. The sites listed here are some of the most helpful ones we've found while researching the jobs in this volume. These sites, which are listed in alphabetical order, are offered for your information. The authors do not endorse any of the information found on these sites.

Action Jobs
http://www.actionjobs.com

While much of the Web site is aimed at people looking for an adventurous job, there are some terrific narratives and real-life stories of people who *have worked in all sorts of exciting and adventurous jobs, everything from tree planting in Alaska to horse wrangling to working as a professional kickboxer. Access to the thousands of job listings costs $39.95 for 90 days.*

All Experts
http://www.allexperts.com

The oldest and largest free Q&A service on the Internet, AllExperts .com has thousands of volunteer experts who can answer your questions on just about anything. You also can read replies to questions asked by other people. Each expert has an online profile to help you pick someone you think might be best suited to answer your question. Very easy to use, it's a great resource for finding experts who can help to answer your questions.

America's Career InfoNet
http://www.acinet.org

This site has a wealth of information! You can get a feel for the general job market; check out wages and trends in a particular state for different jobs; and learn more about the knowledge, skills, abilities, and tasks for specific careers; and learn about required certifications for specific careers and how to get them. In addition, you can search for more than 5,000 scholarships and financial opportunities to help pay for your education. This site also maintains a huge career resources library with links to nearly 6,500 online resources. For fun, you can take a break and watch one of nearly 450 videos featuring real people at work—everything from able seamen to zoologists!

Backdoor Jobs: Short-Term Job Adventures, Summer Jobs, Volunteer Vacations, Work Abroad and More
http://www.backdoorjobs.com

This is the Web site of the popular book by the same name, now in its third edition. While not as extensive as the book, the site still offers a wealth of information for people looking for short-term opportunities: internships, seasonal jobs, volunteer vacations, and work abroad. Job opportunities are classified into several categories: Adventure Jobs, Camps, Ranches & Resort Jobs, Ski Resort Jobs, Jobs in the Great Outdoors, Nature Lover Jobs, Sustainable Living and Farming Work, Artistic & Learning Adventures, Heart Work, and Opportunities Abroad.

Career Guide to Industries
http://www.bls.gov/oco/cg/cgindex.htm

For someone interested in working in a specific industry, but who may be undecided about exactly what career to pursue, this site is the place to start. Put together by the U.S. Department of Labor, you can learn more about the industry, working conditions, employment, occupations (in the industry), training and advancement, earnings, outlook, and sources of additional information.

Career Planning at About.com
http://careerplanning.about.com

Just like most of the other About. com topics, the career-planning area has a wealth of information, together with links to other information on the Web. Among the essentials are career-planning A-to-Z, a career-planning glossary, information on career choices, and a free career-planning class.

Career Prospects in Virginia

http://www3.ccps.virginia.edu/career_prospects/default-search.html

Career Prospects is a database of entries with information about more than 400 careers. Developed by the Virginia Career Resource Network, the online career information resource of the Virginia Department of Education, Office of Career and Technical Education Services, was intended as a source of information about jobs important to Virginia—but it's actually a great source of information for anyone. While some of the information (such as wages, outlook, and requirements) may apply only to Virginia, most details (such as what it's like, getting ahead, skills) and the links will help anyone interested in that career.

Career Voyages

http://www.careervoyages.gov

This "ultimate road trip to career success" is sponsored by the U.S. Department of Labor and the U.S. Department of Education. This site provides specific information in separate sections for students, parents, career changers, and career advisors. The FAQ offers great information about getting started, the high-growth industries, how to find your perfect job, how to make sure you're qualified for the job you want, tips for paying for the training and education you need, and more. Also helpful are the Hot Careers *and the* Emerging Fields *sections.*

Find It! in DOL

http://www.dol.gov/dol/findit.htm

A handy source for finding information at the extensive U.S. Department of Labor Web site. You can Find It! *by broad topic category, or by audience, which includes a section for students.*

Fine Living: *Radical Sabbatical*

http://www.fineliving.com/fine/episode_archive/0,1663,FINE_1413_14,00.html#Series873

The show Radical Sabbatical *on the Fine Living network looks at people willing to take a chance and follow their dreams and passions. The show focuses on individuals between the ages of 20 and 65 who have made the decision to leave successful, lucrative careers to start over, usually in an unconventional career. You can read all about these people and their journeys on the show's Web site.*

Free salary survey reports and cost of living reports

http://www.salaryexpert.com

Based on information from a number of sources, Salary Expert will tell you what kind of salary you can expect to make for a certain job in a certain geographic location. Salary Expert has information on hundreds of jobs—everything from more traditional jobs to some unique, out-of-the-ordinary professions such as acupressurist, blacksmith, denture waxer, taxidermist, and many others. With sections covering schools, crime, community comparison, and community explorer, this Web site is filled with helpful information. You might also find the moving center *a useful site for those who need to relocate for training or employment.*

Fun Jobs
http://www.funjobs.com

Fun Jobs has job listings for adventure, outdoor, and fun jobs at ranches, camps, ski resorts, and more. The job postings have a lot of information about the position, requirements, benefits, and responsibilities so that you know what you are getting into ahead of time. And you can apply online for most of the positions. In addition, the Fun Companies *link will let you look up companies in an A-to-Z listing, or you can search for companies in a specific area or by keyword. The company listings offer you more detailed information about the location, types of jobs available, employment qualifications, and more.*

Girls Can Do
http://www.girlscando.com

"Helping Girls Discover Their Life's Passions," this Web site has opportunities, resources, and lots of other cool stuff for girls ages 8 to 18. Visitors can explore sections on Outdoor Adventure, Sports, My Body, The Arts, Sci-Tech, Change the World, *and* Learn, Earn, and Intern. *In addition to reading about women in all sorts of careers, girls can explore a wide range of opportunities and information that will help them grow into strong, intelligent, capable women.*

Hot Jobs: Career Tools Home
http://www.hotjobs.com/htdocs/tools/index-us.html

While the jobs listed at Hot Jobs are more on the traditional side, the Career Tools *area has a lot of great resources for anyone looking for a job. You'll find information about how to write a resume and a cover letter, how to put together a career portfolio, interviewing tips, links to career assessments, and much more.*

Job descriptions & job details
http://www.job-descriptions.org

Search for descriptions and details for more than 13,000 jobs at this site. You can search for jobs by category or by industry. You'd probably be hard-pressed to find a job that isn't listed here, and you'll probably find lots of jobs you never imagined existed. The descriptions and details are short, but it's interesting and fun, and might lead you to the career of your dreams.

Job Hunter's Bible
http://www.jobhuntersbible.com

This site is the official online supplement to the book What Color Is Your Parachute? A Practical Manual for Job-Hunters and Career-Changers, *and is a great source of information with lots of informative, helpful articles and links to many more resources.*

Job Monkey: Cool summer jobs, seasonal jobs, and year-round careers in the US and Abroad.
http://www.jobmonkey.com

Job Monkey claims to be your gateway to "The Coolest Jobs on Earth," and that they are. Not only can you read all about some of the coolest, most exciting and adventurous jobs in the world, you can search the listings for a really cool job. Job Monkey has listings for summer jobs, seasonal jobs, and full-time jobs around the country and around the world. The Job Hunting Tools *section offers valuable advice to help you land the job of your dreams; of special interest is the* Travel Center. *Caution:*

Most of the jobs at Job Monkey require you to travel.

Job Profiles
http://www.jobprofiles.org
This site offers a collection of profiles in which experienced workers share rewards of their job, stressful parts of the job, basic skills needed, and challenges of the future, together with advice on entering the field. The careers include everything from base-ball ticket manager to pastry chef and much, much more. The hundreds of profiles are arranged by broad category. While most of the profiles are easy to read, you can check out the How to browse JobProfile.org *section (http://www.jobprofiles. org/jphowto.htm) if you have any problems.*

Major Jobs Web Sites at Careers.org
http://www.careers.org/topic/01_jobs_ 10.html

This page at the Careers.org Web site has links for more than 40 of the Web's major job-related Web sites. While you're there, check out the numerous links to additional information.

Monster Jobs
http://www.monster.com
Monster.com is one of the largest, and probably best known, job resource sites on the Internet. It's really one-stop shopping for almost any job-related subject that you can imagine: Find a new job, network, update your resume, improve your skills, plan a job change or relocation, and so much more! Of special interest are the Monster: Cool Careers *(http://change.monster.com/ archives/coolcareers) and* Monster: Job

Profiles (http://jobprofiles.monster.com) sections, where you can read about some really neat careers. The short profiles also include links to additional information. The Monster: Career Advice section (http://content.monster. com) has resume and interviewing advice, message boards where you can network, relocation tools and advice, and more.

Occupational Outlook Handbook
http://www.bls.gov/oco
Published by the U.S. Department of Labor's Bureau of Labor Statistics, the Occupational Outlook Handbook *(sometimes referred to as the OOH) is the premiere source of career information. The book is updated every two years, so you can be assured that the information you are using to help make your decisions is current. The online version is very easy to use; you can search for a specific occupation, browse though a group of related occupations, or look through an alphabetical listing of all the jobs included in the volume. Each of the entries highlights the general nature of the job, working conditions, training and other qualifications, job outlook, average earning, related occupations, and sources of additional information. Each entry covers several pages and is a terrific source to get some great information about a huge variety of jobs.*

The Riley Guide: Employment Opportunities and Job Resources on the Internet
http://www.rileyguide.com
The Riley Guide is an amazing collection of job and career resources.

Unless you're looking for something specific, one of the best ways to maneuver around the site is with the A-to-Z Index. You can find everything from links to careers in enology to information about researching companies and employers. The Riley Guide is a great place to find just about anything you're looking for, and probably lots of things you never dreamed you wanted to know! But be forewarned—it's easy to get lost in the A-to-Z Index, because it's filled with so many interesting things.

USA TODAY Career Focus
http://www.usatoday.com/careers/dream/dreamarc.htm

USA TODAY offers their "dream job" series on this Web site. In these interview profiles, people discuss how they got their dream job, what they enjoy the most about it, describe an average day, their education backgrounds, sacrifices they had to make for their jobs, and more. They also share words of advice for anyone hoping to follow in their footsteps. Most of the articles also feature links where you can find more information. The USATODAY.com Job Center (http://www.usatoday.com/money/jobcenter/front.htm) also has links to lots of resources and additional information.

CAREER TESTS AND INVENTORIES

If you have no idea what career is right for you, there are many resources available online that you can use to categorize your interests and steer you in the right direction. While some of the assessments charge a fee, many others are free. You can locate more tests and inventories by searching for the keywords career tests, career inventories, or personality inventories. Some of the most popular assessments available online are:

Campbell Interest and Skill Survey (CISS)
http://www.usnews.com/usnews/edu/careers/ccciss.htm

Career Explorer
http://careerexplorer.net/aptitude.asp

Career Focus 2000 Interest Inventory
http://www.iccweb.com/careerfocus

Career Maze
http://www.careermaze.com/home.asp?licensee=CareerMaze

Career Tests at CareerPlanner.com
http://www.careerplanner.com

CAREERLINK Inventory
http://www.mpc.edu/cl/cl.htm

FOCUS
http://www.focuscareer.com

Keirsey Temperament Test
http://www.keirsey.com

Motivational Appraisal of Personal Potential (MAPP)
http://www.assessment.com

Myers-Briggs Personality Type
http://www.personalitypathways.com/type_inventory.html

Skills Profiler
http://www.acinet.org/acinet/skills_home.asp

The Career Interests Game
http://career.missouri.edu/students/
explore/thecareerinterestsgame.php

The Career Key
http://www.careerkey.org

Princeton Review Career Quiz
http://www.princetonreview.com/cte/
quiz/default.asp

READ MORE ABOUT IT

The following sources and books may help you learn more about adventuresome careers.

GENERAL

Camenson, Blythe. *People Working in Service Businesses.* Lincolnwood, Ill.: VGM Career Horizons, 1997.

Cohen, Paul and Shari. *Careers in Law Enforcement and Security.* New York: The Rosen Publishing Group, Inc., 1995.

Culbreath, Alice N. and Saundra K. Neal. *Testing the Waters: A Teen's Guide to Career Exploration.* New York: JRC Consulting, 1999.

Dawicki, Ed. *Adventures Unlimited: The Guide for Short-Term Jobs in Exotic Places.* Lincoln, Neb.: iUniverse, 2003.

Doyle, Kevin. *The Complete Guide to Environmental Careers in the 21st Century.* Washington, D.C.: Island Press, 1998.

Echaore-McDavid, Susan. *Career Opportunities in Law Enforcement, Security, and Protective Services.* New York: Checkmark Books, 2000.

Farr, Michael, LaVerne L. Ludden, and Laurence Shatkin. *200 Best Jobs for College Graduates.* Indianapolis, Ind.: Jist Publishing, 2003.

Fasulo, Mike and Jane Kinney. *Careers for Environmental Types & Others Who Respect the Earth.* New York: McGraw-Hill, 2001.

Fogg, Neeta, Paul Harrington, and Thomas Harrington. *College Majors Handbook with Real Career Paths and Payoffs: The Actual Jobs, Earnings, and Trends for Graduates of 60 College Majors.* Indianapolis, Ind.: Jist Publishing, 2004.

Henderson, C.J. and Jack Dolphin. *Career Opportunities in the Armed Forces.* New York: Checkmark Books, 2003.

Hiam, Alex and Susan Angle. *Adventure Careers: Your Guide to Exciting Jobs, Uncommon Occupations and Extraordinary Experiences.* 2nd ed. Franklin Lakes, N.J.: Career Press, 1995.

Jakubiak, Joyce, ed. *Specialty Occupational Outlook: Trade and Technical.* Detroit: Gale Research, Inc., 1996.

Krannich, Ronald L and Caryl Rae Krannich. *The Best Jobs for the 1990s and into the 21st Century.* Manassas Park, Va.: Impact Publications, 1995.

Lee, Mary Price, Richard S. Lee, and Carol Beam. *100 Best Careers in Crime Fighting.* New York: Macmillan, 1998.

Mannion, James. *The Everything Alternative Careers Book: Leave the Office Behind and Embark on a New Adventure.* Boston: Adams, 2004.

Miller, Louise. *Careers for Nature Lovers & Other Outdoor Types.* New York: McGraw Hill, 2001.

Quintana, Debra. *100 Jobs in the Environment.* New York: Macmillan, 1996.

Stinchcomb, James. *Opportunities in Law Enforcement and Criminal Justice.* Lincolnwoood, Ill.: NTC/VGM, 1996.

Stone, Kendall. *Rope, Ride, Ranch & Rodeo: A way of life in the San Bernardino Mountains.* Yucca Valley, Calif.: K.J. Stone, 1990.

ADVENTURE TRAVEL GUIDE

Turner, Cherie. *Adventure Tour Guides: Life on Extreme Outdoor Adventures.* New York: Rosen Publishing Group, 2003.

ADVENTURE TRAVEL WRITER

Dial, Cynthia. *Teach Yourself Travel Writing*. New York: McGraw-Hill, 2001.

Farewell, Susan. *How to Make a Living As a Travel Writer*. New York: Marlowe & Co., 1997.

O'Neal, L. Peat. *Travel Writing*. Cincinnati: Writers' Digest Books, 2000.

AIR TRAFFIC CONTROLLER

Maples, Wallace. *Adventures in Aerospace Careers*. New York: McGraw-Hill, 2002.

ARCHEOLOGIST

Camenson, Blythe. *Opportunities in Museum Careers*. New York: McGraw-Hill, 1999.

———. *Careers for History Buffs & Others Who Learn from the Past*. 2nd ed. New York: McGraw-Hill, 2002.

Echaore-McDavid, Susan. *Career Opportunities in Science*. New York: Checkmark Books, 2003.

BULL RIDER

Stone, Kendall. *Rope, Ride, Ranch & Rodeo: A way of life in the San Bernardino Mountains*. Yucca Valley, Calif.: K.J. Stone, 1990.

COAST GUARD OFFICER

Henderson, C.J. and Jack Dolphin. *Career Opportunities in the Armed Forces*. New York: Checkmark Books, 2003.

Paradis, Adrian A. *Opportunities in Military Careers*. New York: McGraw-Hill, 1999.

CYBERSLEUTH

Campen, Alan D., Douglas H. Dearth, and R. Homas Goodden, eds. *Cyberwar: Security, Strategy, and Conflict in the Information Age*. Fairfax, Va.: AFCEA International Press, 1996.

Hafner, Katie and John Markoff. *Cypberpunk: Outlaws and Hackers on the Computer Frontier*. New York: Simon and Schuster, 1991.

Hoffman, Lance J., ed. *Rogue Programs: Viruses, Worms, and Trojan Horses*. New York: Von Nostrant Reinhold, 1991.

Hutt, Arthur E., Seymour Bosworth, and Douglas B. Hoyt, eds. *Computer Security Handbook*. New York: John Wiley & Sons, 1995.

Icove, David, Karl Seger, and William Von Storch. *Computer Crime*. Sebastopol, Calif.: O'Reilly and Associates, 1995.

National Research Council. *Computers at Risk: Safe Computing in the Information Age*. Washington, D.C.: National Academy Press, 1991.

Quarantiello, Laure E. *Cyber Crime: How to Protect Yourself from Criminals*. Lake Geneva, Wisc.: Limelight Books, 1997.

Rosenbaltt, Kenneth S. *High-Technology Crime: Investigating Cases Involving Computers*. San Jose, Calif.: KSK Publications, 1995.

Shimomura, Tsutomu and John Markoff. *Takedown: The Pursuit and Capture of Kevin Mitnick, America's Most Wanted Computer Outlaw—By the Man Who Did It*. New York: Hyperion, 1996.

Stair, Lila B. *Careers in Computers*. Lincolnwood, Ill.: VGM Career Horizons, 1996.

FBI SPECIAL AGENT

Fisher, David. *Hard Evidence: How Detectives Inside the FBI's Sci-Crime Lab Have Helped Solve America's*

Toughest Cases. New York: Simon &
  Schuster, 1995.
Jeffreys, Diarmuid. *The Bureau: Inside
  the Modern FBI*. Boston: Houghton
  Mifflin, 1995.
Kessler, David. *The FBI: Inside the World's
  Most Powerful Law Enforcement
  Agency*. New York: Pocket Books, 1993.
Thomas, Ralph D. *How to Investigate
  by Computer*. Austin, Tex.: Thomas
  Investigative Publications, Inc., 1998.

HELICOPTER TRAFFIC REPORTER

Goldberg, Jan. *Opportunities in
  Entertainment Careers*. New York:
  McGraw-Hill, 1999.
Tuggle, C.A. *Broadcast News Handbook:
  Writing, Reporting, and Producing*.
  New York: McGraw-Hill, 2000.
White, Ted. *Broadcast News Writing, Repor-
  ting, and Producing*. 3rd ed. Boston: Focal
  Press, 2001.

LOBSTERMAN

Corson, Trevor. *The Secret Life of Lobsters:
  How Fishermen and Scientists Are
  Unraveling the Mysteries of Our
  Favorite Crustacean*. New York:
  HarperCollins, 2004.

MOUNTAIN GUIDE

American Red Cross. *Emergency Response*.
  St. Louis: Mosby Lifeline, 1997.
American Rescue Dog Association. *Search
  and Rescue Dogs: Training Methods*.
  New York: Howell Book House, 1991.
Fox, Deborah. *People at Work in Mountain
  Rescue*. Parsippany, N.J.: Silver Burdett,
  1996.
Hempel, John C. and Steven Hudson,
  eds. *Manual of U.S. Cave Rescue
  Techniques*. Huntsville, Ala.: National
  Cave Rescue Commission, 1988.
Tilton, Buck. *Rescue from the Backcountry:
  Basic Essentials*. Merrillville, Ind.: ICS
  Books, 1990.

NAVY SEAL

Henderson, C.J. and Jack Dolphin. *Career
  Opportunities in the Armed Forces*.
  New York: Checkmark Books, 2003.
Paradis, Adrian A. *Opportunities in
  Military Careers*. New York: McGraw-
  Hill, 1999.

PRIVATE INVESTIGATOR

Akin, Richard H. *The Private Investigator's
  Basic Manual*. Springfield, Ill.: Charles
  C. Thomas Publisher, 1979.
Anderson, Kingdon Peter. *Undercover
  Operations: A Manual for the Private
  Investigator*. Boulder, Colo.: Paladin
  Press, 1998.
Dempsey, John S. *An Introduction to Public
  and Private Investigations*. Minneapolis/
  St. Paul: West Publishing Co., 1996.
Golec, Anthony M. *Techniques of Legal
  Investigation*. Springfield, Ill.: Charles
  C. Thomas Publisher, 1995.

PYROTECHNICIAN

Drews, John M. *Making a Living in Fire-
  works*. American Fireworks News, 1994.
Greenspon, Jaq. *Careers for Film Buffs &
  Other Hollywood Types*. Lincolnwood,
  Ill.: VGM Career Books, 1993.

RODEO CLOWN

Stone, Kendall. *Rope, Ride, Ranch &
  Rodeo: A way of life in the San
  Bernardino Mountains*. Yucca Valley,
  Calif.: K.J. Stone, 1990.

SMOKEJUMPER

Beyer, Mike. *Smokejumpers: Life Fighting Fires*. New York: Rosen Publishing Group, 2001.

Delsohn , Steve. *The Fire Inside: Firefighters Talk about their Lives*. New York: HarperCollins, 1996.

Landau, Elaine. *Smokejumpers*. Brookfield, Conn.: Milbrook Press, 2002.

Masi, Mary and Lauren Starkey. *Firefighter Career Starter*. 2nd ed. New York: Learning Express, 2001.

Mudd-Ruth, Maria. *Firefighting: Behind the Scenes*. Boston: Houghton Mifflin, 1998.

Narramore, Randy. *How to Prepare for an Interview and Obtain a Job as a Firefighter*. Public Safety Publications, 1994.

Paul, Caroline. *Fighting Fire*. New York: St. Martin's Press, 1998.

Pyne, Stephen and Patricia Andrews. *Introduction to Wildland Fire*. New York: Wiley & Sons, 1996.

VOLCANO CHASER

Fisher, Richard V. *Out of the Crater*. Princeton, N.J.: Princeton University Press, 1998.

Hayhurst, Chris. *Volcanologists: Life Exploring Volcanoes*. New York: Rosen Publishing Group, 2002.

WHITE-WATER RAFTING GUIDE

Ray, Slim. *Swiftwater Rescue: A Manual for the Rescue Professional*. Asheville, N.C.: CFS Press, 1997.

INDEX